Live, lead & fail Quickly!

12 SECOND CULTURE

SPEED IS THE CURRENCY OF BUSINESS. IS YOUR TEAM FAST ENOUGH?

Mike Metcalf & Shaun Peet
with Stephen Copeland

12 Second Culture
Speed is the Currency of Business. Is Your Team Fast Enough?
www.12secondculturebook.com
www.deckleadership.com

Copyright © 2020 by Mike Metcalf & Shaun Peet

Published by The Core Media Group, Inc.,
P.O. Box 2037, Indian Trail, NC 28079
www.thecoremediagroup.com

Cover & Interior Design by Nadia Guy.

Photos provided by Mike Metcalf, Shaun Peet, and Shutterstock/Avigator Fortuner.

ISBN 978-1-950465-37-8

All rights reserved. No part of this publication may be reproduced, stored in a retrieval system, or transmitted in any form or by any means — electronic, mechanical, photocopy, recording, or any other — except for brief quotation in printed reviews, without the prior written permission of the publisher.

Published in the United States of America.

Table of Contents

Note to the Reader: The Myth Distilled 05
1 - The Department of Unrealistic Expectations 09
2 - Fail Quickly 17
3 - Arrival Mindset 35
4 - Prove People Right 47
5 - Winning with Good People 59
6 - Diversity Isn't Just a Black or White Issue 71
7 - Creating Environment 85
8 - Vertical Thinking 105
9 - Inspiring Great Efforts 123
10 - P=W/T 139
11 - Everything Matters 155
12 - Kindness Wins 165
About the Authors 179

Note to the Reader: The Myth Distilled

Distillation | *di-stə-ˈlā-shən (noun)*
The action of purifying a liquid; the extraction of the essential meaning or most important aspects of something.

The National Association of Stock Car Automobile Racing, America's premier motorsports organization, known to many as NASCAR, was largely a by-product of adrenaline-crazed bootleggers who possessed an adept talent for souping up factory automobiles and driving them through twisting Appalachian Mountain roads in an effort to elude law enforcement. In the backwoods of the South, locals would unload the moonshine for a day to gather their steel stallions and put on a high-octane show.

But while the show was going on around makeshift racetracks, the main event was happening in the shadows: moonshiners, bootleggers, and runners were swapping products and secrets and planning their next steps. In the heart of the defiant South, these men didn't take too kindly to Uncle Sam's limitations of speed or prohibition. So the show went on. What a spectator would see was a *distraction* of what was actually going on.

Moonshine can be made only through distillation. Ingredients are gathered and then purified over time under both intense heat and intense cooling. Moonshine done well is smooth, clear, and very powerful—words we seldom use to describe work, social environments, or organizational cultures.

We believe a distillation of sorts, as it relates to our careers, needs to occur for the sustainability of our work environments and ultimately our society. Our goal is not to save the American workplace; that will be up to you! Our aim, rather, is twofold: first, to distill the myth that suggests that our lives, our families, and our environments are in a good place as long as we are racing up the ladder and attaining financial security (the myth of success) and second, to reconstruct a foundation for workplace cultures that will liberate and inspire the human soul.

Simply put, winning (or advancing) at all costs is killing us.

It's time for a change.

Consider the following statistics:

- Heart attack rates are highest on Monday mornings.
- More than 50 percent of US employees would trust a complete stranger over their boss.
- About two-thirds of US employees lack *engagement* (the connection or inspiration people experience in their work).

We will stop here, but all of this points to the brokenness of the environment that most of us are currently experiencing. The American Dream is a race to the top and seems to lead more toward oppression than elevation. Distilled, it shifts our attention away from what is happening in front of our eyes. This dream facilitates "leaders" who hire people who often look and think like them, limiting the beauty of *diversity*; who compromise change and *efficiency* in the name of tradition; who stunt the growth of healthy *culture* for the sake of control; and, finally, who are so immersed in the process that there is no time for *kindness* to the people sustaining the process. *The result is a draining work environment leading to real lives that are marred with stress and anxiety.* As educator and author Deborah Meier states, "People only burn out when they are treated like appliances."

You should know that we're not anyone special in the world's eyes.

We don't claim to have all the answers. We're not big-time executives. We don't oversee Fortune 500 companies. We're pit-crew coaches. But in the world of racing—which is all about speed, efficiency, and performance—we've been quite surprised to see just how much our message resonates with people in all corners of the American workplace.

In our cutthroat industry, we've seen misery fester beneath poor leadership, and it has inspired us to lead and play our part in creating healthy work environments. We didn't enter racing to climb the corporate ladder into positions of leadership. It found us. We have said "yes" to the call and are now blown away by where we are asked to speak and by whom we are consulted to come in and help, whether it's small businesses like Well Krafted Roofing and Lineberger Orthodontics or big businesses like Novant Health, Colonial Life Insurance, Meritor, Merck Pharmaceuticals, and the Kansas City Chiefs. What we are saying is not unique; it's just been mostly forgotten in the race for success. We're passionate about significantly improving those heartbreaking statistics we referenced earlier and jump-starting the change we want to see in leaders and in organizations.

It's why we started DECK Leadership. DECK is an acronym for *diversity, efficiency, culture,* and *kindness.* All our programming ideology is driven from these four cornerstones, and we believe a focus on executing these well will result in an increase in connection, performance, and fulfillment.

We wrote this book for everyone, young and old, women and men, and all those in between. Though racing has historically been male-dominated, there are now a number of female drivers, crew members, executives, and mechanics. Our hope is to see women play a larger role in the sport, especially in the Cup Series, the highest level of racing. Diversity will continue to bloom if we can keep shifting more from the ego to the soul, both individually and collectively. That's certainly one of the many positive things that Millennials have brought into the workforce: their hearts. They let their voices be heard. With all their oft-reported flaws, they don't easily settle and are carried along by their passion. Of course, this can also make them challenging to coach. But thanks to their help, we believe we have learned how to effectively coach them. They make up the largest percentage of our workforce in pitting race cars. In fact, it was a Millennial who was the catalyst for turning our pit-crew culture around after several stints on different racing teams. Many of the principles in this book will help bridge the gap between young up-and-comers and seasoned veterans in the workforce, hopefully inspiring people of all ages to reunite around certain values that can move cultures forward.

Again, moonshine done well is clear, smooth, and very strong. Trust us on that. When diversity, efficiency, culture, and kindness (DECK) are done well, the same can be said about our workplaces and the world we give to our future generations. We're passionate about working alongside companies, organizations, and teams—and helping them establish a DECK foundation that will move their culture forward.

It's time for a massive shift in our environment. It's time to shift the narrative of the American Dream. What if the race isn't a solo run to achieve your dream but a collective race to help others achieve theirs? It will take relentless work and selflessness, but what if *you*, reader, were the one who helped distill it for us all?

Opportunity is endless. The world is waiting for you to act.

The Department of Unrealistic Expectations

The race car, traveling at a speed of 55 miles per hour, comes to a screeching halt. The jack man leaps from the pit wall in front of the speeding race car to lift a 3,400-pound race car with one stroke of the jack. The tire changers sprint to the right side of the car, slide to their knees, and pull the trigger on 200 pounds of air that will result in 1,200 RPM spinning through a pneumatic air gun, which they use to engage the first of five lug nuts. The carrier runs in front of the car, delivers a 65-pound tire to the jackman, and moves toward the right rear of the car. The gasman engages a 95-pound can of fuel into a fuel coupler to begin refueling.

-The 1st second in a NASCAR (National Association of Stock Car Auto Racing) pit stop

We've had a heck of a night, we thought. *We deserve to win this thing.* But as brilliant of a night of pit stops that our pit crew had displayed, it looked like we would fall just short. On a humid September evening in Richmond, Virginia, Martin Truex Jr., our main rival and points leader, had driven a dominating car to a seemingly insurmountable lead in the Federated Auto Parts 400. With only four laps remaining, victory was all but assured. But assurances in NASCAR are thinly veiled, and just as our driver, who was in second place, keyed up his radio to say, "It would be cool to get a caution right now," a loud boom resonated over the deafening horsepower that blanketed the Richmond International Raceway. Driver Derrick Cope, in the No. 15 car, had blown a tire, resulting in a full-field caution signaled by a waving yellow flag.

Our elation was quickly tempered by the reality that our crew chief would most certainly make the call to come down pit road and change four tires. Our hearts raced. We knew we had to control the emotion of the moment. If we were fast and executed our pit stop, we knew we had a chance to win. But it would require flawless execution.

Truex's pit crew, after all, was one of the best on pit road. Staffed by NASCAR powerhouse Joe Gibbs Racing, they were a highly skilled, highly paid, veteran unit that was rarely beat off pit road. They were the equivalent of the New York Yankees. We, on the other hand, had half the pit-crew budget of Truex, and people in our own company lovingly referred to our team as the "Island of Misfit Toys." We would have to change four tires in less than 12 seconds to have any shot at beating Truex off pit road.

As the cars came off Turn Four under the yellow caution flag, one by one, all the lead lap cars followed each other onto pit road, nose to tail. They were trying to give their respective crews every advantage in hopes of gaining valuable positions coming out of the pits.

Our crew chief came over the radio and counted our driver into the pit box: "Ten away…five, four, three, two, one, foot on the brake, wheel straight…"

Go time.

Our crew attacked Kyle Larson's skidding race car with a ferocity that the moment required. The scream of the pit guns engaging the lug nuts signaled the start. Our pit crew changed right-side tires effortlessly and transitioned around the car. We knew we had a chance.

Our jackman then blazed around the car and threw his 27-pound jack under the 3,400-pound race car and lifted it with a single, hard-won stroke of the handle. As the car lifted off the ground, both changers pulled the tires off the car in unison, instantaneously replacing them with two new Goodyear racing tires. The parallel cadence of the pit guns hitting five lug nuts was the signal for the jackman to drop the car.

The Department of Unrealistic Expectations

Done.

The ear-splitting noise and tire smoke from the car launching out of the pit stall concluded the pit stop. It was quick. Actually, it was really quick, and we knew we had a chance to take the lead off pit road.

We eyed the video monitor on a massive scoring pylon that towered above the infield garages. Truex was still in his pit stall when Larson passed him on pit road.

As celebratory comments came across the radio, we knew our guys had done it. They had taken the lead off pit road and put our driver in a position to win the race. They had changed four tires and emptied one can of fuel into the car in 10.2 seconds, besting Truex's pit crew's time of 11.7. Larson, considered one of the top young talents in the sport, did the rest. He nailed the restart and drove the Target Chevrolet to a lead he would not relinquish.

During Larson's memorable race-winning burnout, time seemed to slow for us. We watched our guys celebrate their victory. As their pit crew coaches, we couldn't help but feel a sense of pride in seeing the joy they displayed in victory, having witnessed firsthand all their hard work.

Our front-tire changer and both tire carriers had all been fired from their previous teams.

Our jackman was told he was only good enough to exist in a backup role.

And our rear-tire changer, not even two years into his career, was thought to be on pit road way too early in his development to be able to handle the pressure of this exact situation.

They each might have been making far less money than those in their respective positions on other race teams, and they might have had far less experience comparatively, but culture had become a competitive advantage and carried them to victory on that day.

This was not a moment that came easily to us. It was the product of a multitude of mistakes and long days, framed by a tireless dedication to get it right and create a culture of excellence. We believe culture can become a competitive advantage for you, too. This is our story.

According to Richard Petty, the recognized king of NASCAR, racing started "the day they built the second automobile." And from that very moment, the drive to go faster and the need to get to the finish line first has been all-consuming.

For decades, the focus on speed has been on the cars. Increased horsepower, sleeker bodies that slip through the air, and tricked-out fuel systems were all innovative improvements that led drivers to victory lane. However, as NASCAR continued to implement rules aimed at leveling the playing field, the engineering advantage diminished. The cars were so close in performance on the racetrack that teams had to look elsewhere to claim a competitive advantage. Their gaze turned to pit road and the opportunity to win positions in the pits.

Ever since the inception of the sport, a team of mechanics would wrench on the car all weekend, and when race day came, they would switch roles and perform the pit stops. There was a paradigm shift in the mid-1990s, when racing teams began replacing their mechanics with specialists: guys whose only job was to focus on their specific task on the pit crew. Many of these "specialists" were former athletes.

This began with Jeff Gordon's pit crew under crew chief Ray Evernham in the mid-90s, known as the "Rainbow Warriors," a group of athletes who spent about half their workday pitting race cars and the other half wrenching on race cars. This transition from mechanics to athletes paid immediate dividends, dropping pit-stop times from 30 seconds to under 20 seconds. The move to training athletes to pit race cars made sense. Athletes could lift, move, and be coached in a way that mechanics could not. Most had also been exposed to the pressure-filled moments that were sure to arise. The success of the Rainbow Warriors forced teams to follow suit, and the new mold across NASCAR became hiring athletes for their pit crews.

Thirteen years later, another transition took place. Red Bull Racing entered NASCAR and recruited the first group of athletes who had *full-time* pit crew responsibilities and no race-shop responsibilities. Instead of turning wrenches, they were turning their focus to pit stops for ten hours a day. That's how we—a former football player and hockey player, a "black guy" and a "Canadian," two of the first fourteen athletes recruited by Red Bull—accidentally found a home in the sport of NASCAR.

Red Bull Racing's willingness to implement innovative strategies and blow up the constructs of tradition was very formative for us. We drew inspiration from this for our own program years later. They showed us a better way.

It was during this era that pit-stop times slowly began to drop again, to around 11 seconds. Since the 1980s, pit stops had gone from in excess of one minute to under 12 seconds. But with this transition brought an entirely new, perfectionistic desire for efficiency—times that were no longer measured in seconds but rather in tenths of seconds. Suddenly, every single movement mattered. Like most industries, as processes evolved, so did the need for high-performing, efficient cultures. With this intense pressure to perform, however, also came an array of problems: these evolving processes and the rush to be fast led to devaluing the people who were completing these processes.

At that time, the role of a pit crew coach was still in its infancy. Pit crew coaches had been around for only a few years, and not every team employed one. This led teams to rush to fill the position, and the result was half disastrous, half comical, and rarely successful. The tendency was for teams to hire macho-type men with some previous connection to sports who were more interested in being a "coach" of a professional sports team than leading people. We heard a story about one coach who, in an effort to inspire his tire-changer, told him in a particularly important moment that he should approach this pit stop as though his little girl's life was on the line. There was another coach who laid claim to founding the United States Navy SEALs and creating Crossfit. All this to say, we've both witnessed this kind of ridiculousness over the course of our careers and have been on the business end of thoughtless tirades, runaway emotions, and absolute absurdity.

Nobody we know grew up aspiring to be a NASCAR pit crew coach. To be honest, neither of us even knew NASCAR teams had coaches. We both got involved in NASCAR through a serendipitous chain of events and introductions that set the course for our involvement in a sport neither of us knew much about. So, after navigating the ups and downs of our first decade in motorsports, we became coaches out of a desire to see it done a better way.

As NASCAR pit-crew coaches, it is our job to assemble and train one of the most efficient sectors of teams in the world.

"How efficient?" you might ask. "And "Really? In the *world?*"

We're not exaggerating. We're in charge of a team of five people who can change four tires on, and add two cans of fuel to a race car in 12 seconds. What can you do in *12* seconds? Are you able to tie your shoes?

Efficiency is absolutely key for each member of the pit-crew team:

1. The **fueler**, who must tote a 95-pound can of fuel on his shoulder and plug it into a skidding race car in under 1 second. If all goes well, the car leaves pit road full of fuel. If it goes badly, he's a human torch.
2. The **jackman**, whose job is to lift a 3,200-pound race car with one stroke of the jack. To begin his job, he must jump in front of a race car traveling upwards of 55 miles per hour to get to the far side of the car. Do you remember when you were growing up and your parents told you not to play in traffic? Yeah, forget about that. If you want to know what this feels like, go out to the Interstate, put your heels on the white line with your back to the traffic, and let the evening rush hour blow past you just inches away. If that doesn't unnerve you, you may have what it takes to be a jackman or jackwoman. (Madison Ferguson, the only female to ever hold this position, competed in the truck series for a few seasons and did a phenomenal job.)
3. The **tire carrier**, who must deliver two 65-pound tires to the right side of the car and mount one of the aforementioned tires on a hub in under 0.8 seconds. Have you ever rotated the tires on your car or truck and you heaved the wheel up on to the hub and rotated it until the holes lined up with the studs? It's like that but different.
4. And finally, there are two **tire changers** who are tasked with hitting five lug nuts in under a second. Quick math on this equates to two-tenths of a second per lug nut. If you're wondering how fast two-tenths of a second is, blink your eyes once. That's two-tenths of a second, and in the world of NASCAR, it's an eternity. You might be wondering how two-tenths can be all that import-

ant. The math reveals the magnitude. The cars are traveling on the racetrack at 190 mph, so two-tenths of a second at 190 mph equals a distance of 56 feet. The difference of 56 feet at the Daytona 500 is the difference between finishing *first* and finishing *sixth*. The difference in prize money between first and sixth is $1.1 million. And the most amazing part? *All this is expected to happen every single time the car comes down pit road, without fail.*

The sheer magnitude of the amount of money that is on the line for every race that is won or lost by tenths of seconds requires almost constant perfection. It is for this reason we laughingly refer to our department as "The Department of Unrealistic (but Achievable) Expectations."

Perhaps you can relate to being expected to do something that feels as if it's on the edge of what is humanly possible. You might be able to relate to the high demands for efficiency and performance your superiors place on you. It's a demand that most in the American workplace easily become enslaved to, a demand that often dictates the mood of leaders, and a demand that affects the overall health of a workplace environment. When there is a good performance, the workplace is bearable. When there is a bad performance, the workplace is miserable. This fickle nature of most work environments hinging on performance often produces efforts birthed out of fear rather than inspiration.

Though we are in a business where a small mistake resulting in the loss of two-tenths of a second can cost a million dollars, we have chosen to lead differently and shift the focus to developing *culture* rather than obsessing over *performance*.

Do you feel underfunded, under-resourced, under-appreciated, or under pressure? So do we. Maybe you're a teacher who is expected to improve the scores of your students' standardized tests, but your kids do not even have the necessary school supplies. Or maybe you're a manager expected to meet a certain quota, but your team members hate their jobs or the owner of the company. The list goes on…

Despite the demands raining down from up top or the unforeseen challenges that arise in uncontrollable situations, there is always an opportunity for leaders to create a healthy culture for those they are leading—so they can thrive as workers, but most importantly, grow as people. When you have a healthy environment, the unthinkable is possible.

As is said in NASCAR, as the race is about to start, "Pull them belts tight." The green flag is out, and we are going racing.

Fail Quickly

The race car remains jacked up in the air with only its left-side tires in contact with pit road. The jackman locates a piece of tape signaling the correct spoke to grab the wheel of the soon-to-be-installed right-front tire. The tire changers have removed all five lug nuts in order to pull a 65-pound wheel from the hub, often with one hand. Locating a point an inch away from the mid-calf of the kneeling tire changer, the carrier arrives at the right rear of the car, ready to hang the new tire. The gasman empties the first four gallons into the car.

-The 2nd second of a NASCAR pit stop

Even casual NASCAR fans can tell when there is a horrible pit stop. If they had any doubt, then the crew chief spiking his headset onto the diamond plate of the pit box is a dead giveaway.

It was a night when we were racing on one of NASCAR's biggest stages: the annual All-Star Race at the Charlotte Motor Speedway, an eighty-lap shootout where the winner collects a $1 million check. With a race this short in duration, we would get only three attempts to pit the race car.

So far, we were 0-for-1. In the first stop, our rear tire changer had experienced a jammed lug nut in his socket, which cost him valuable time and resulted in us losing six positions as the car returned to the racetrack. Just as our tire changer finished his explanation of what happened, I (Peet) turned to find myself nose-to-nose with the crew chief. He was visibly upset, or, as we like to say in NASCAR, "spittin' mad."

"Forget about winning one million!" he screamed as the owner of the team observed with equal disgust. "We aren't even going to be able to win five cents if we keep this up!"

Having made his point, he climbed back up to the pit box. I made reservations for his anger, but it did not change what we were doing. Our misstep on the first pit stop was an anomaly, and this was a capable group. In addition, we had two more pit stops to perform, and our guys were ready. They had been coached to fail quickly from the very moment we sat down together as a group in January. Whatever had slowed us down in the first stop was examined, deconstructed for any teaching moments, and quickly thrown away. We had to maintain the confidence required of the task, and that was possible only if we failed quickly.

Our final opportunity of the night came with just ten laps remaining. Our driver was in fourth place, and to have any shot at winning the million dollars, he would have to restart on the front row, either in first or second place. Our objective was clear. Focused, not mired in their earlier failure, our pit crew laid down the fastest stop of the race. The car gained the necessary two spots it needed to restart on the outside of row one. After a brilliant restart, we took the lead and the eventual checkered flag. We were millionaires! Or at least a big part of helping our racing team earn the million dollars.

Sitting on the pit box that night was former Carolina Panthers Head Coach Ron Rivera, the guest of one of the minority owners of the team, Felix Sabates. In Coach Rivera's own words, the pit crew that night went from being relevant to setting a standard to becoming the standard—the very best on pit road. Months later, he would bring that same pit crew in for a season-opening staff-and player-meeting for the 2014 football season to echo those same sentiments. "We were relevant last year, and we can set a standard this year with the goal of *being* the standard in the National Football League," he stated emphatically. The Panthers would go on to make a late sprint into the playoffs in 2014 and then go on a historic run in the 2015 season, which included a trip to the Super Bowl. We share this detail only because you never know how your courage to overcome failure might impact or inspire someone else.

Standing behind the victory-lane stage and watching our guys celebrate the win, it was hard not to be struck with a profound sense of accomplishment. But not over the pit stop that won the race. We are witness to fast stops like that in practice all week long and expect that every Sunday at the track. Honestly, the most satisfying part of this win was how our team met failure and moved past it to create a successful outcome.

One thing we had experienced throughout our NASCAR careers as a jackman (Peet) and a gasman (Metcalf) was that fear was ever-present within the minds of pit crew members. This fear was born out of cultures where nothing was placed above performance and perfection. They were cultures where a pit crew member's worth was only tied to his performance on any given pit stop. The problem with this model is that the NASCAR season is a long, grueling thirty-nine-week schedule that can wear down the most resilient athlete. When fear enters into the day-to-day for this length of time, you have a recipe for burnout. Fear is a cheap source of fuel. When it is the primary source of fuel, breakdown is imminent. Reframing fear as it relates to failure is key to overriding the angst and stress we feel from the never-ending demands of the workplace.

Dismantling the Power of Fear

When we became pit crew coaches, one of our main "culture goals" was to dismantle this fear. We wanted to create a culture where high-performing teams could thrive. We knew our teams didn't have the budget, experience, or facilities to match the other teams, but it was not about *having* the best of everything. If we could, instead, *make the best* of everything, we had a puncher's chance of knocking off the big teams. We identified fear and apprehension as the biggest roadblocks to creativity, brilliance, and fulfillment.

We first joined forces at Red Bull Racing. We enjoyed every single day of pitting race cars those five years. We didn't think it could get any better—that is, until Red Bull announced it was shutting the team down to focus on its Formula 1 racing efforts. We were fortunate that as Red Bull Racing shuttered its NASCAR operation, Michael Waltrip

Racing (MWR) was expanding, adding a third car to their stable. We both signed contracts and were quickly assigned as the new gasman and jackman on Clint Bowyer's 5-Hour Energy Toyota Camry. In addition to our race-day duties, we began coaching in the truck and Xfinity Series and doing consulting work with external businesses. Neither of us sought the position of pit crew coach. Actually, we both turned down the initial opportunities to coach because it would require a lot more time on top of our already demanding jobs.

I (Metcalf) remember walking past the pit crew area where Kyle Busch Motorsports' three pit crews were scheduled to practice. The guys were standing attentively as if they were waiting for instructions. Long story short, they had just learned that their coach had resigned. They asked if I would coach them. I replied that I had too much to do at the time.

"Well, who is going to lead us, then?" one of them asked.

That question stayed with me. I found myself conjuring up all kinds of excuses in my head as I wrestled with the call to lead. I didn't think I was the best candidate for the job. I knew all the positions but had never thought about them holistically. I had never built a team or hired or fired anyone. Yet seeing the eyes of those men that day impacted me. For a few days, I wrestled with haunting questions like: *Who is going to help them achieve their dreams? Do I have time to lead these guys? Am I good enough to coach?* I wasn't sure, but I didn't let my fear get the best of me that week. I didn't want to say yes, but I was unable to say no. I've never looked back. Ironically, as fate would have it, Shaun has an eerily similar story with a different truck/Xfinity team.

A year later, the team we are currently with approached us about taking over their Cup Series pit crews, the highest level of racing. This was an incredibly difficult decision because we had just gotten into a rhythm at MWR. Our team had three of the top ten crews in NASCAR's Cup Series, and the crews were winning races and having fun doing it. The pit crews we were coaching were also starting to show promise. In less than a year', one of NASCAR's most unlikely pairings had emerged as leaders—not just in the pit department but also as "glue for the whole organization." However, the teams we coached competed against each other, while this was a chance to work together. We started our journey as teammates, but a brotherhood was emerging, and this was our shot.

In both cases, we knew that if we failed as coaches, it wouldn't mean we were failures but that we would regroup and simply have to find another avenue to achieve desired outcomes helping others achieve success. In the last six months of 2011 (Red Bull) and 2013 (MWR), rumors began to fly that the team might shut down. As you can imagine, fear ran rampant in an already fear-based environment. We decided to fight against this fear. How? We settled on focusing on growth over performance. It's not what you earn but what you learn. The joy was in the experience, the lessons, and the things we can control, not in our performance. As we began coaching, we disconnected our sense of worth and purpose from what we would get out of coaching and entrusted our worth into what we were willing to put into it.

Fear of failing always seems to be the elephant in the room—that thing that is always in the way of doing what you want to do or going where you need to go. Each of us has gifts we want to share with the world, but fear of failing blocks us from intentionally pursuing those desires and living out our authentic lives.

Part of fear is human nature: it taught our ancestors to run from bears, avoid jumping off cliffs, and keep fires contained. It is also perfectly, naturally "human" to be afraid to try new things because we fear that our plans may fail. But fear becomes amplified when it is part of the DNA of a workplace environment—when people try to instill fear in those below them as a way to manipulate or control them. Manufacturing fear is all about the ego; it's a way to flex strength and power and convince oneself that he or she is important because of his or her position or status. Many workplaces are dominated by this type of fear. Often these fears are simply projected downward, all the way through the chain of command, spiraling through each stage of hierarchy. Creativity, innovation, and efficiency thrive in freedom, but there's little freedom when someone is terrified of failing.

Whenever that fear of failure is being projected downward in our company, we've committed ourselves to making it stop at us. We will not perpetuate the cycle of fear-mongering. Our guys put enough pressure on themselves attempting to get the race car on and off pit road as fast as humanly possible. In an environment like ours that is extremely performance-driven and judged by others through the lens of deci-seconds, there is no room to play small.

That's why we constantly preach to our team to *fail quickly*.

"Fail" and "quickly" are two words that don't usually find each other side-by-side in the English language. *Failure* is synonymous with negative outcomes and is obviously viewed as bad. *Quickness* in our industry is viewed favorably because speed wins races. Remember, we are tasked with changing four tires and putting two cans of fuel in a race car in 12 seconds. We operate on the edge of what is humanly possible and in constant pursuit of perfection. We know failure is coming. However, our success at the racetrack is not based on whether or not we fail but rather *how quickly* we can navigate those failures and get back to optimizing our performance. We accomplish this by failing quickly.

If we have a tire changer who misses hitting the first lug nut, we want that tire changer to fail quickly and hit the next five succinctly. If we have a jackman who fails to lift the car properly on the right side, we ask him to fail quickly and retreat to fundamentals while running around the car to jack up the left side. Or if we fail to execute on the first stop of the race, we ask our team to fail quickly and be great on the next stop. Do you see the pattern?

Attempting anything challenging in life is going to involve failure. But why are we so blindsided by it when it happens? There are a lot of people with mounting anxiety in different industries today because their approach to work doesn't incorporate failure. They become rattled when something goes wrong, and their natural response is to either micromanage a situation until their exhaustion forces them to give up or perhaps to just give up altogether because their identity is so closely tied to their performance. The first step, when blindsided by failure or met by an unexpected challenge, is to dive into it instead of giving up. Failure is almost always the **First Act In Learning** and a catalyst for growth.

By imploring our guys to fail quickly, we can reframe failure and the way they view it. By allowing them to fail quickly, we create a type of cognitive cradle for each of them so they do not fear failure. Instead, they integrate it. They know they have the space to fail, but if they do fail, then they need to do it quickly. They know to extract any positives or teaching moments from the failure and move past it. This approach creates mental freedom, which leads to efficiency in their work. Because they know they *can* fail and that we will have their backs when they *do* fail, what we've found is that they'll swing for the fences and give their all in the pursuit of excellence. If you want to develop a healthy environment, you have to start by deconstructing the narrative—the fear of failure—that dominates most workplaces, and more importantly, that space between our ears.

We once heard a story about a leader who asked his team to take out a sheet of paper. He told them they had five minutes to write down anything they would do currently or in the future if they had infinite boldness and courage. One minute into the exercise, he stopped them all and informed them that if they had anything written on their papers—anything—it was fear keeping that dream from becoming a reality, not a lack of boldness. Anything written down was doable, if one is willing to confront the fear.

Win or Learn

A few years into our tenure as pit crew coaches in the Cup Series, a number of people within our company were frustrated because our race team couldn't seem to get over the hump and win races. We were close to winning, week in and week out. But just couldn't seem to find our way into victory lane.

Late one evening, we were wrapping up an extended film session at the race shop when a senior executive sought us out to discuss his frustration with being unable to win. We were able to pinpoint two dominant attitudes that were negatively affecting the company: the feeling of complacency and the feeling of being cursed.

There was a complacency in the mindset of some in the company—a sort of country-club mentality where people felt safe and secure knowing that the team was performing well enough to hold onto its main sponsor, who had been the title sponsor for more than a decade.

But those on the opposite side of the spectrum desperately wanted to win and felt that our team was cursed because we had come so close to winning so many times. There were, after all, some odd things that had unfolded in the company. Without going into the details, within a couple of years, some incredibly unfortunate events had occurred among team members and within the company. As for the current season, many felt like we had everything we needed to get to victory lane—the sponsors, the drivers, the mechanics, and the pit crew—and wondered what it would take to finally turn the page—from good to great, from competitive to elite. But out of this victimized mentality, we could see that many within the company were beginning to focus on what we *didn't* have: the budget, the superstars, the experience, etc.

As we discussed these dominant attitudes with our boss, we had a thought: What if we reframed our mindset when we didn't win? Instead of viewing those races as failures, what if we focused on what we could learn from each race we didn't win? A young developmental tire changer who was watching film with us interjected and challenged our boss: "So, what are our options moving forward?" Everyone already knew the answer as our boss confidently replied, "To win or to learn."

It was clear that this should be the team mantra and that we ought to carry that mantra with us into every practice and every race weekend. We all loved this subtle mental switch so much that we created a banner to hang in the race shop with these three words: *Win or learn*.

Winning is a process that would take more than our fair share of time and a lot of learning. In fact, every time a certain executive from one of our sponsors would see the banner, he would say to us, "You guys aren't winning much, so you must be the smartest guys in NASCAR." He even went so far as to start addressing us as "Doctor."

All jokes aside, these three words, "Win or learn"—when truly applied—positioned our men to fail quickly. Again, it created that cognitive cradle—that safe space for them to be fearless and give their full effort—that stripped failure of its sting.

Most view their efforts through the lens of results, critically categorizing their efforts in either a W (Win) or L (Loss) column. In the workplace, so much time is wasted dwelling on past performances. That drains people of their energy and motivation in the present and further paralyzes their hope for the future. But we believed that if we could get our guys to transition from the frustration and negativity associated with "Loss" to the opportunity and growth associated with "Learn," we felt we would be better positioned mentally to be a high-performing team. After all, if you think your efforts are cursed, then you're not failing quickly. "Failing quickly" propels us forward. In other words, your efforts are like spinning tires: no matter how rough or torn the surface is, if there is propulsion, movement is imminent.

We decided to focus our attention on what we could control and to develop an insatiable appetite for learning and growing, which reframed failure. Learning redeemed losing because the growth opportunity in failing propelled us forward. In a sense, it propelled us forward in a way that winning never could.

Failure Is Just a Stop along the Way

To fully position yourself to adopt a growth-focused mindset—a healthier, more integrated approach to failure that involves learning from each setback—you have to identify the origin of your fear of failure.

Most people's fear of failure is birthed in their own egos. Ego-driven people tend to be less successful over time than people who are task-oriented or goal-oriented. Ego-driven people slide more rapidly into condescending or negative self-talk because of their disappointment in themselves or their performance, which leads to an often all-consuming fear of failure. This fear hovers over them like a cloud, and their performance often dictates their moods and sense of purpose.

Reacting to this overwhelming fear of failure (perhaps through micromanagement, anger, or fear-based tactics) might sometimes lead to short-term success, but it hardly ever leads to long-term success. Long-term success involves developing a culture that transcends fear. Clear-thinking, goal-oriented people realize that their route to completion is a process—filled with ups and downs, successes and failures, and, overall, lots of learning.

When your ego isn't calling the shots, you can more easily realize that failure does not dictate who you are or who your team is. Failure is simply just a stop along the way. It's not your final destination or where you get off. The train keeps moving. Often, in fact, failure is the catalyst that will get you where you wanted to go all along because of something that you or your team will learn in that failure. Therefore, failure isn't to be feared; it is to be embraced. That's usually where all the opportunity for growth resides.

It hurts to experience failure. We're not downplaying the painfulness of that experience. But whenever you begin to associate failure with your worth, or whenever failure in one particular aspect of your life begins to intrude on other aspects of your life or the present moment that deserves your full attention, it might be worth asking these questions:

1. Why am I allowing this failure to cut me so deeply?
2. What is the lie that this failure is telling me about myself?
3. What does this failure teach me about myself, my profession, and the industry I'm in?
4. What can I personally learn from this failure, and how can I use what I have learned to lead others or help others?
5. What specifically about this failure is painful?
6. What steps can I take so that this is a little less painful the next time a failure like this occurs?

We once worked on a crew where one tire changer was loved and another was hated. They were similar in talent and work ethic and had made a similar number of mistakes. The only difference is that one always owned up to his shortcomings and was committed to improving, while the other blamed everything and everyone but himself. Again, failure isn't the end; it doesn't have to define you. So you don't have to run from it. Don't make excuses to yourself or to others about the failures or mistakes you've made. Excuses only appease the people who make them. Acknowledge it, and move on.

Growth Mindset

We worked with a tire carrier years ago who was a perfect fit for our team because of how he responded to a disastrous mistake. His resolve under duress and how he rebounded from his mistakes made him a valuable member of our team. Very early in his racing career, adversity showed up in a big way. With only a few laps to go in a big race, the car was heading, unscheduled, into the pits. The car was out of gas.

This was before fuel injection in stock car racing, so the crew chief asked for someone to spray ether in the cowl of the hood to get the car to quickly refire when the gasman plugged his can into the side of the car. The tire carrier volunteered. He felt that this was his moment to assert himself as a leader, as someone who was ready to act and deliver. He wasn't just a jock doing this racing thing for fun; he wanted to show people that he belonged. And he did just that—but in the wrong place. He sprayed ether not into the airbox just above the motor but into the

NACA duct that supplied air to the driver's helmet. The car refired, and the driver returned to the racetrack, nearly driving through the outside retaining wall of Turn 4 due to excessive fume inhalation. From hero to zero. Everyone's day was over.

Making mistakes can be embarrassing, especially preventable mistakes. Had he done a little more research or asked for direction, the results would have been different. They may not have won the race, but at least he wouldn't have been the cause of wrecking a $200,000+ race car.

For years, this particular failure inspired him to tell that story to other young crew guys so they wouldn't make similar mistakes in their development. His failure was an opportunity for improvement for himself and many others. Also, the car had an Energizer battery sponsor. The story was told so many times that, for the remainder of his career, this carrier was affectionately referred to as the "Ether Bunny."

This is what failing quickly and growth mindset are all about. He accepted that he made a mistake, did what he could to make up for it, moved on from that mistake, learned from it, and created something new and beneficial to our team and organization out of that space of failure. He also didn't take himself too seriously and welcomed his new nickname.

Growth mindset affects the way you develop and grow throughout your life because if you simply see failure as a speed bump—a learning experience, something that is part of the process of discovering your best self—you will roll with the punches and position yourself to truly succeed. We have another quote hanging in our gym that emphasizes this idea: "The only time you must not fail is the last time you try."

In psychologist Carol Dweck's brilliant book, *Mindset: The New Psychology of Success*, she says the two dominant types of thinking are "fixed mindset" and "growth mindset." People with a fixed mindset are all about image and believe their intelligence is static. They desire to look smart and therefore have a tendency to avoid challenges, give up too early when faced with obstacles, see their efforts as fruitless (or worse, ignore useful and negative feedback), and feel threatened by others' successes. People with a growth mindset, on the other hand, are all about learning, believing their intelligence can be developed. They desire to grow and therefore have a tendency to embrace challenges, persist in the face of setbacks, see their efforts as the path to mastery, learn from criticism, and find lessons and inspiration in the success of others.[1]

Dweck compares the thought processes of people with a fixed mindset with those of people with a growth mindset. She says both groups monitor what's going on, but people with a fixed mindset associate something good that led to a positive result or something bad that led to a strong negative label. About people who have a growth mindset, Dweck writes, "Their internal dialogue is not about judging themselves and others in this way. Certainly they're sensitive to positive and negative information, but they're attuned to its implications for learning and constructive action... 'What can I learn from this? How can I improve?'"[2]

Believing that your qualities are carved in stone—the fixed mindset—creates an urgency to prove yourself over and over. It manufacturers desperation and insecurity. After all, if you have only a certain amount of intelligence, a certain personality, and a certain moral character...well, then you'd better prove that you have a healthy dose of them. It simply wouldn't be beneficial to look or feel deficient in these most basic characteristics.

But with a growth mindset, these traits are not simply a hand you're dealt and have to live with. By adopting a mindset that is all about personal growth, you're not always trying to convince yourself and others that you have a royal flush when you're secretly worried it's a pair of tens. Suddenly, the hand you're dealt is just the starting point for development. This growth mindset is based on the belief that your basic qualities are things you can cultivate through your efforts. Although people differ in every which way—in their initial talents and aptitudes, interests, or temperaments—everyone can change and grow through application and experience.

We use a growth mindset to develop and reinforce the fundamental skills that determine our success. For example, if our guys go out and

---

[1] "Fixed vs. Growth: The Two Basic Mindsets That Shape Our Lives," Maria Popova, Brain Pickings, September 23, 2018, https://www.brainpickings.org/2014/01/29/carol-dweck-mindset/.
[2] Carol S. Dweck, PhD, Mindset: *The New Psychology of Success* (New York: Ballantine Books, reprint, updated edition, December 26, 2007), 225.

run a 12-second pit stop, we don't just pat them on the back and tell them, "Good job." We would be doing them a massive disservice if we were to do this because we would not be leaving them with anything valuable for growth. Instead, after they run a 12-second pit stop, we try to highlight the points of execution that led to the fast stop. In place of a brief moment of adulation, we point out to them that when their hand angle is correct and they set the tire a certain way, it allows us to run a 12-second stop. If we manage our pace and our breathing, we can run a 12-second stop. If our tire changers hit lug nuts hard and we can minimize the time it takes from our last lug nut hit to the time we drop the car off the jack, we can run a 12-second stop. It is only after we reinforce these fundamentals that we tell them, "Good job." By doing this, we reinforce the execution of the skills that lead to fast pit stops.

Failure is coming, and it can either stun you, which isn't the least bit efficient, or it can serve you as part of the process that gets you where you want to be. Growth mindset brings with it a perspective that helps you avoid sinking too low in struggles and instead inspires you to confront challenges, insecurities, and mistakes head-on. Dweck talks about the danger of falling into the binary trap of "success" or "failure;" however, the vastness between those two ideas is where real learning and growth unfolds. You either succeed at what you're trying to do, which is rewarding, or you learn something valuable, which is also rewarding. It's a win–win. It's emotional efficiency. Adversity is a gateway to growth: that's the psychological frame that someone with growth mindset operates within, positioning him or her to fail quickly and learn a lot along the way while pursuing excellence.

Ability to Pivot

Fear of failure often arises whenever people are faced with change or uncertainty. Growth mindset is especially vital when in a phase of unknowing.

For example, heading into the 2018 NASCAR season, we found out that pit crews would go from six starters to five starters, just as they had gone from seven to six a few years before. This was as massive a transition as it would be for the NBA to go from five players on the court to four. Our entire strategy was affected. Cuts would have to be made. We would have to change the way we approached just about everything at practice and on race day.

The first thing we did to help extinguish the fear that came along with all the uncertainties we were facing was communicate honestly with our guys. Lack of communication can make the unknowns especially terrifying. People's careers and sense of stability, after all, were at stake. The least that leaders can do during a transition is to communicate openly and honestly with those they are leading. No one likes to feel like they are scrambling around in the dark. So we addressed every unknown we could, and anything we couldn't address, we told our team we would work to find answers. A leader's ability to reduce uncertainty is imperative because uncertainty is often where fear abounds.

Pivoting, and the ability to change direction, requires courage and innovation. We knew that the new skill set that was demanded of them could lead to failure, but we also knew that how we introduced that change to our team—how we unearthed all the unknowns around it—could also give us an edge over every other pit crew that was navigating that same change. So, instead of coming up with our own strategies for our team to execute as coaches, we divided them into groups and asked them to come up with strategies about how to change four tires and fuel a race car quickly with one man less. All of a sudden, they were taking on the unknown themselves, which built confidence and understanding in their ability to pivot. Then each group shared that strategy and why they felt it was a good plan of attack. This process might have involved more failing and experimenting, but it was also more thorough, helpful, and collaborative.

In a recent article in *The Washington Post*, entrepreneur and professor Jonathan Aberman said this about pivoting: "In the arc of a career or a business, inevitability of success does not exist. It requires hard work, some luck and the match between demand for what you have and your ability to provide it. Some fortunate people have a path that never wavers and the demand and supply match-up occurs and is sustained. However, for most of us, somewhere along the way we must modify our path and pivot to get there."[3]

[3.] "To Improve Your Odds of Success, Master the Pivot," Jonathan Aberman, *The Washington Post*, January 30, 2017, https://www.washingtonpost.com/news/capital-business/wp/2017/01/30/to-improve-your-odds-of-success-master-the-pivot/.

When change and unknowns fell upon us, we communicated the challenge that had come down the line, made sure our team knew we would be there for them and with them as we navigated that challenge, and then committed ourselves to being the very best at tackling that challenge. Whenever faced with pivoting, failing quickly is especially important because these series of quick failures will inspire your new direction.

Run toward the Fire

We recently had two guys on our team who couldn't be more different on paper. One was a white guy, Phil, from the wealthy southeast side of Charlotte, who came from a rock-solid family. The other was a black guy, Will, from the westside of Charlotte, whose family was in a different environment entirely. Phil had a lot of opportunities growing up. Will had very few. Both have athletic backgrounds. Both joined our pit crew at the same time. Both were competing for the same position.

The two of them frequently seemed to bump heads on certain things but always seemed to put up with one another. One day, however, there was an explosion. Phil had just recently outpaced Will and moved up onto a Cup Series pit crew, while Will stayed on a developmental crew in the minors. Will took a playful jab at Phil after a rough practice, and it caught him at the wrong time. Phil responded by saying, "How about you make it onto a Cup car before you worry about what I'm doing?!"

Not one to back down from a challenge, Will responded by saying, "Well, it's going to be tough for you to pit that Cup car on Sunday from the hospital."

"We don't solve our problems here by fighting. If you touch me, you'll get fired!"

"Well, if you think that me getting fired gives you the right to talk to me like that, you have another thing coming," Will responded.

At that point, they were nose to nose, neither backing down.

In the meantime, one of the crew guys ran into our office and said, "Hey, you might want to get outside! Will and Phil are about to go at it, and I'm not sure how long the rest of us can keep things from getting out of control."

So we quickly went outside and simply said, "You two, inside, *now!*"

We sat them down, asked who wanted to share his side of the story first, and assured them that none of us were leaving the room until the dispute was settled.

Tempers flared again. We tried to mediate the conversation while letting each man say exactly what he wanted to say.

By the end of the conversation, each of them had a deeper understanding for one another's temperaments and personalities. They learned that they both had a short fuse at work because they were tested more than others on the team. Phil learned more about Will's background and why he might be sensitive to a white guy making the kind of comments he made about being looked down on. And Will learned more about Phil's background and realized that he wasn't like some of the other guys who had frustrated him in the past.

"What you might not realize," Phil eventually said to Will, "is that I am one of your biggest cheerleaders here. I try to work behind the scenes and help you out as much as possible. Nothing would make me happier than to see your success—to see you on one of the Cup cars."

The two of them eventually embraced, and to this day, they are one another's biggest supporters on the team. There are still misunderstandings. They both still have sensitivities. But that conversation changed everything for them. It was a special moment to see their names on the leader board as our top two carriers to start the 2019 year at the Daytona 500, both on Cup cars.

People in the workplace often mistakenly believe that conflict means failure, which makes people fear conflict all the more. When this kind of fear dominates an environment, people find themselves walking on eggshells, internalizing their frustrations, and taking their anger out on other things or people—often outside of work. But disagreements aren't failure. Conflict isn't failure. Tension isn't failure. Failing quickly is all about diving into the tension, not avoiding it, and running toward the fire. Sometimes that fire does involve a mistake or failure of some sort. Sometimes tension entails someone being in the wrong. But acting like the fire isn't there never gets rid of the fire. Bad leaders let a fire burn until it dies down, thinking that just because there's no longer a fire, peace has returned. Smoldering embers can ignite quickly if not completely quenched. The truth, however, is that a fire—no matter how big or small—leaves wreckage.

Part of failing quickly is reframing conflict. Whenever there is tension, there is an opportunity for understanding and awareness—for growth. Communicating in tension can lead to awareness, which leads to a shared experience, which leads to unity. Your team can actually benefit from tension when it is approached the right way. It's an opportunity. Tension unlocks doors and provides direction for conversations.

Will you have the courage to push the door open?

Arrival Mindset

The race car remains jacked up in the air with only its left side tires in contact with pit road. The jackman hangs the right front tire on the car. From the moment he initiates movement to the time the tire is mounted on the car is less than 0.8 seconds. The tire changers set the tires they pull off the car so that they do not roll out onto pit road and switch their button on the gun from "off" to "on." The carrier begins to index the right-rear tire. The gasman empties gallons five through seven into the car.

-The 3rd second of a NASCAR pit stop

The view you adopt for yourself profoundly affects the way you live your life. Every single one of us has a choice in how we show up. At home. At work. And in life. We challenge the *arrival mindset* of our pit crew athletes from the moment they begin working with us.

So what exactly is an arrival mindset? It is a collection of your thoughts and corresponding attitudes that steer your behavior the exact moment you grab the door handle and move through the door that leads to work. We demand that our teammates show up as the very best version of themselves every day. The version that is the hardest working, the most collaborative, the most innovative, the most coachable...you get the idea. We hang such a heavy emphasis on mindset because mindset steers everything. You may have an incredible strategy or develop a championship plan, but if you don't have a team with the mindset to execute that plan, it will likely fall short. We want our guys to arrive engaged. Just like engaging a transmission, movement is not possible without engagement. Our success starts with our mindset.

We all, however, are familiar with a different story as it pertains to arrival mindset. Consider this perhaps all-too-common scenario. A company employee groggily wakes up in the morning. The only thing that can possibly help her bear the dread she feels on this morning is a cup of coffee, so she goes to a nearby coffee shop and waits in line to buy an overpriced coffee. She eventually arrives at work disengaged, walks through the doors, and goes straight to her assigned work space. As the morning unfolds, she begins counting down the minutes to her lunch break. She stretches her lunch break to the very last minute, dreading the reality that her day is only halfway over. And then she returns to her office to plow away once more, which she dutifully does. Finally, at five o'clock on the dot, she leaves and blends into the stampede of fellow coworkers celebrating their release from the workday. It's a workday devoid of joy. But it pays the bills, and it's better, she thinks, to have her humanity stripped away and to be reduced to a number for forty hours a week than it is to be unemployed. So she deals with it. And then the next day, she will do it all over again.

Uninspired environments lead to a lack of intention in people's arrival mindsets. Most people we talk to express a common theme about their employment: they feel that all they have to offer their bosses and their company is their time. Not their thoughts. Not their ideas. Not their passion. Not the fullness of their energy or their personality. *Just their time.* Most feel unheard, trapped in a role where they have very little to offer. Just a task to complete at their boss's demands so they can collect a paycheck and insurance.

Where did we get the idea that the workplace should be miserable and difficult? For some reason, many bosses falsely think that if those below them are having fun or laughing or enjoying themselves, they cannot possibly be productive. So, once again, as discussed in the previous chapter, fear reigns. And many higher-ups implement this fear or misery in the name of productivity. The result is the opening anecdote: employees simply going through the motions, often at the sake of their own sanity. Their arrival mindset—their mental state when stepping into another day—is simply to survive the day, disengaged.

But even if you find yourself in an uninspired environment that isn't your fault, what if you attempted to reframe your mindset? After all, each of us throughout our lives is challenged to approach the negative or challenging situations that come our way with a mindset that is both healthy and purposeful. What if the morning commute was a way to meditate, reflect, and prepare for an amazing day? What if getting the overpriced coffee was a chance to interact and connect with another human who, like you, needs to feel alive and that he or she matters? What if work wasn't just about a job or a career but about a calling? When we infuse our mindset with love and hope, it's difficult to groggily wake up, fly out of the house, try to outsmart everyone on the highway, overpay for coffee, and arrive at work focused simply on a to-do list.

No matter the kind of environment you are in, your arrival mindset is the first and most important decision of your workday! Similar to a pace-setter for a runner trying to achieve a goal, your mindset allows you to keep pace with your intentions. Most people's misery, apathy, or lack of inspiration in the workplace is often related to the environment they are in.

We've heard it said, "When a flower doesn't bloom, you fix the environment in which it grows, not the flower." Although this might be true, it is external. Simply put, you still have a major role to play. For an organization to thrive, leadership needs to be strong at *every* level, which means we *all* have a role to play. Environments are best changed from the inside out, by leading from the middle (which we will dive into more in chapter 9). Our arrival mindset creates space for us to flourish in our environment.

"It's Crush Time"

Despite the high-octane energy on display each Sunday during race season, with the screaming post-anthem fighter jets and the roar of forty 600 HP engines at the start of the race, the racing industry throughout the week at the office probably doesn't look much different than any other corporate environment. In our experience on different race teams, the shop often has a fear-based, performance-driven sterility to the environment, which allows misery to fester. Produce or you are out.

What we learned at our first racing team together, however, was that we could create our own culture, within our own group, no matter how cold the overall environment. We had each assumed, upon getting into racing, that we probably wouldn't ever have as much fun as we had in our athletic careers. But working at Red Bull Racing proved that notion wrong. Being on that team and attempting something new in the industry as the first-ever full-time pit crew members was innovative and inspiring.

This idea of intentionally adopting the right arrival mindset is demonstrated by two of the big-culture guys we worked with on Red Bull's pit crew. Because we didn't have our own gym at Red Bull, we had to work out at the local YMCA, located in a wealthy lakeside community. These workouts usually took place at about ten o'clock in the morning, when the YMCA was crawling with soccer moms. We had two massive, former football players on our team who were in the middle of a beard-growing contest. Before their workout, they would both make their way to the top of the stairs, stand there amid all the moms, strangely face one another, nose-to-nose and then scream at the peak of their lungs, "*It's crush time!*" as spit flew in their faces.

As comically disruptive as this was, it also had a way of getting each pit crew member in the right frame of mind. On the days that we hadn't quite shaken the morning off or were worn out and dreading the coming intensity of our workout, these goofballs gave us something to not only look forward to but also a mindset to replicate. Screaming "*It's crush time!*" at each other was the perfect picture of both intentionality and presence. They rooted themselves in the moment and dedicated themselves, through this absurd display, to the workout—a perfect mix of fun and passion. It was obvious to everyone that they were there to give their maximum effort. And it inspired everyone else's maximum effort, reminding each person that each day is an opportunity to bring something within themselves that could uniquely contribute to the culture.

Every large company has an environment—something of a corporate ecosystem—but within that environment a wide range of cultures can be found, depending on the leaders of each group or department. A company has as many different cultures as it has managers. The culture within our pit crew was inspiring and enjoyable. Rarely do you hear someone say, "I can't wait to go to work," but that was exactly how we felt each day. People on our team were reluctant to take vacation days for fear of missing out on the continuation of something that happened the day before. It was like being back in the locker room: filled with camaraderie and laughter, but centered around hard work and competition. This fun and enjoyable culture positioned each pit crew member to enter each day with the right arrival mindset.

A culture can influence someone's arrival mindset, but it's ultimately up to each person to adopt the right mindset for himself or herself. Life as a pit crew member involves hard work, intense scrutiny, and extreme focus. Whereas someone in accounting might be able to come to work hungover midweek and coast through the day from the confines of a cubicle, there's no "off-days" as a pit crew member. (We had a young changer come in hung over once, and we did pit stops until he saw only five lug nuts per wheel—not the ten he started swinging for when practice began.) Between the difficult early-morning workouts and the countless practice pit stops where your coaches meticulously evaluate every little move you make, being in a pit crew requires your full presence and intentionality.

How you start your day often dictates your potential for effectiveness. And how you start your day will dictate how you sustain your day.

A motivated inexperienced employee will give you a lot more than an unmotivated but experienced employee every time. We bet on people with passion more than we bet on talent. Passion comes from authentically owning whatever it is that excites you. Adopting the right arrival mindset is about challenging yourself to create a culture where the mindset is primed before you come in the door. Your arrival mindset dictates exactly how you will utilize the day. Today you are going to get better, or you are going to get worse.

The choice is yours.

"The Road from Good to Great Is the Steepest Road There Is"

In Angela Duckworth's book *Grit: The Power of Passion and Perseverance*, she tells a brilliant parable about three tradesmen who are in the midst of a large construction project.[4]

[4.] Angela Duckworth, *Grit: The Power of Passion and Perseverance* (New York: Scribner, 2018), 149.

A curious onlooker walks up to the tradesmen and asks the first guy, "What're you guys doing here?"

The man looks at him and says, "I'm laying bricks."

Not satisfied with the answer, he approaches the second tradesman and again asks, "What're you guys doing here?"

The tradesman responds, "I'm building a church."

Wanting a bit more information, the man then asks the third tradesman, "What're you guys doing here?"

The guy pauses and then says to him, "I am building a house of God."

The first guy, Duckworth says, has a job; the second guy has a career; and the third guy has a calling.

So who is going to exhibit the most passion and resilience in the workplace? Obviously, the one who feels that he or she has a calling. And if you are just doing your job, you are missing out on your calling. Your approach to the workday—your arrival mindset—positions you to experience a deep sense of meaning and purpose. The moment you put your hand on the door when you arrive at work, we can usually see if you are going to have a successful day or not. Your arrival mindset sets you up for success.

We have a sign on the door that leads out to practice that reads as follows:

The Road from Good to Great Is the Steepest Road There Is

> It's too steep for the entitled.
> Too challenging for the selfish.
> Too long for the uncommitted.
> Too narrow for the distracted.
> There is only one path to the summit.
> Bring your best self, every day, every pit stop.
> It's *you* vs. *yesterday*.

This is our version of Notre Dame's "Play Like a Champion" banner hanging above their locker-room stairwell or Appalachian State's wooden cut-out that says, "Today I Give My All for Appalachian State." The saying on our door that leads out to practice is a way to remind our team that their presence there, each day, is about more than just surviving the day; it's about aspiring to be the very best version of themselves in the pursuit of human brilliance. If we can distill fear and cultivate courage within our environment so that our group views each setback as an opportunity to grow, then arriving with the right mindset each day is sustainable.

Preparation

During our second off-season, we identified our need to improve the jackman position on one of our cars. To our seemingly good fortune, we were able to sign a jackman who was thought to be one of the best young talents on pit row.

The first opportunity we had to watch him as part of our team came at the season opening Xfinity race (NASCAR's Triple A equivalent) the day before the world-famous Daytona 500. To our dismay, our newly acquired jackman made a disastrous mental mistake for which the car incurred a one-lap penalty. Though we were all disappointed, we didn't think anything of it and wrote it off as "opening-day jitters."

The next day, at the Daytona 500 Cup Series race, which is basically the equivalent of our Super Bowl because of the hype, this jackman approached us after the national anthem, right before the race was about to start. He said to us, "I don't have any jack handles in the pit stall." This was a significant piece of equipment, and it was his responsibility to set it up *before* the race. He should have addressed it by that point in the day.

Another mental error.

We once again began to wonder if we had made a mistake in acquiring this superstar. We were paying him handsomely, after all, and he had made two mental errors in one weekend. The first weekend! His performance during the race was flawless, but his mental errors were a cause for concern.

The second race of the year was at the Atlanta Motor Speedway for the Folds of Honor QuikTrip 500. The car he had pitted the previous week in Daytona had switched sponsors. Along with this switch came a significant change to the paint scheme. Instead of a bright red car with a bullseye on the hood, the car would be bright purple, to match the cleaning product that was being advertised on the race car. During the fourth caution flag in Atlanta, we were racing in the top ten. As the car came down pit road, everybody went out to pit the race car...that is, except for the jackman.

He was looking for the red car with the bullseye—even though he had already jacked the purple car three times during that race!

A third mental error.

It was a reflection of a complete lack of awareness. A lack of intention in getting his mind where it needed to be. Even if, for some reason, he had forgotten what the car looked like, he should have known what position his driver was in and been able to prepare. After the pit stop, he said to us, "I forgot it was the purple car today."

We knew we needed to make changes immediately.

Your arrival mindset is a conscious decision and commitment that has to be made. The hardest part isn't arriving as your best self but rather *making the choice* to arrive as your best self. Yes, for yourself, but most importantly for your teammates. Whereas you can't always control what unfolds in your performance, what you can control is how you position yourself to excel.

In the 2016 season, we had another young jackman who was backing up our hardest-working and most consistent guy on our team, our starter. We could tell one day that our young jackman seemed a little flat and frustrated. We asked him what was going on, and he told us that he felt stuck in his position as a backup. He felt like he was never going to get to the level where he'd be competitive with the person above him; he felt he'd never legitimately be considered for the starting position. While meeting him where he was and hearing his frustrations, we also challenged him and told him that life doesn't reward coasting, and neither does our department—that his teammates needed him to keep approaching each day with intention and passion. We assured him that good things would happen if he stayed the course.

Two weeks later, we raced in Watkins Glen, New York, the only racetrack in the circuit where cars turn right instead of left. This means that we pit the car coming into the pit stall from the opposite direction, reversing all our typical movements. Long story short, our star jackman ripped a calf muscle exploding off his opposite leg to approach the car and was lost for the race. Insert the youngster.

For the rest of that race and several after, he filled in flawlessly for our superstar—one of the best jackmen in racing—and we didn't miss a beat. It was his arrival mindset—a shift from being status-focused to presence- and excellence-focused—that prepared him for his opportunity to fill in and allowed him to succeed. Had he been coasting, he likely would have felt unprepared to rise to the occasion.

Hard work always pays off, whether it is through filling in for a starter or inspiring your fellow teammates in practice. But work ethic begins with how you think and how you arrive day after day after day. It was a special moment for us as coaches to celebrate our young jackman's success after the Watkins Glen race. "I'm so glad we had that talk a few weeks ago," he said with a thunderous smile!

Often, we are closest to breaking through at the time when we want to throw in the towel. The resistance we experience when our goals are within sight is just the universe conspiring against us to see how badly we want to achieve those goals. Arrive as if today will be the day that everyone will understand how brilliant, positive, energetic, and talented you are.

Shoot For the Moon

There's a parable we use at the beginning of every new season as a way to relate perspective to our group. The parable is about a guy who has been through a pretty rough patch in his life. His girlfriend left him, his dog died, and he just found out that he lost his job. In short, this guy is a country song. With no more options and no one left to turn to, out of desperation he drops to his knees beside his bed and prays to the Lord, "I can no longer shoulder the weight of the cross I have to bear; it's just too heavy."

To the man's good fortune, the Lord appears before him and says, "If you can't handle the weight of the cross you have been asked to bear, I will allow you to trade it for another. Come with me."

So the Lord takes the man away, and they arrive at a room that is filled with thousands of different crosses: iron crosses, stone crosses, wooden crosses, massive crosses, tiny crosses, crosses of all sizes. The Lord then looks at the man and says, "If the cross that you have been asked to bear is too heavy for you, I will allow you to pick a new one." The man is ecstatic; he knows this could be the big break that makes life easier. He takes his time scouring the room, thinking about how easy his life is going to be once he finds the smallest cross.

After a couple of hours searching, he finds a cross made of two toothpicks banded together by a piece of string. He picks it up, and it is as light as a feather. He excitedly runs to the front of the room where the Lord is waiting for him. Nearly out of breath from his excitement, he tells the Lord, "After a lot of care and deliberation, I have found the cross I'd like to bear." The Lord looks down at the cross and then up at the man and responds, "Um, you can't have that one."

Dumbfounded and defeated, the man replies, "But I thought you said I could have any cross I wanted."

The Lord then says, "Yes, I did, but that's the one you brought in here."

We relate this parable to our team in an attempt to reveal to them that some of the things they are complaining about pale in comparison to what others are experiencing. And that the heft of the cross we are being asked to bear might not be quite as heavy as we believe it to be. After all, we are grown adults who get to play with race cars for a living. How bad do we really have it?

Your arrival mindset doesn't affect only your own effort; it also affects the efforts of others. Showing up at work and complaining about how awful your life is because the barista messed up your latte not only allows negative energy into the workplace, but it could pale in comparison to the difficulties a fellow coworker might be struggling with. Imagine complaining about something as insignificant as your morning coffee order to a coworker whose spouse was just diagnosed with cancer. You never know the heft of the cross that each person is asked to bear.

If you come through the door when you first get to work talking about how tired you feel or how much you hate your job or how unfair your boss is, people don't want to be around you. People generally aren't drawn to those whose posture is negative or victimizing. People want to be around others who uplift them or make them into better people. People intuitively know when they are around those who have contagious energy. It's only in negativity that people are recruited into cycles of gossiping and viewing the glass as half-empty. People inherently want to be inspired and all prefer hope over despair.

The Saturn V rocket that launched humans to the moon weighed

6.2 million pounds at lift-off. Two minutes and forty-two seconds into the flight, 76 percent of the fuel was needed to escape the earth's gravitational pull—that's 4.7 million pounds of propellant in just under three minutes. There is a calculated thrust needed from the very start to get beyond the Earth's atmosphere (roughly sixty-two miles) into space. Simply put, the energy created at the start gives the entire journey a chance.

You, too, get to decide what kind of energy you expend as you launch into the day. Each of us must shift our mentality from always answering the performance-driven question of, "What will it take for me to get as much accomplished as possible today?" to the relationship-driven and intrinsic question of, "What is the best way for me to start this day for myself and my team?" Don't survive your day; thriving starts with arriving.

4

Prove People Right

The jackman returns to the jack, watching for both changers to finish reinstalling the right-side lug nuts. The tire changers finish installing lug nuts on the right side tires. The carrier steps around the rear changer to grab the old right-rear tire in his right arm. The gasman empties gallons seven through nine into the fuel cell.

-The 4th second of a NASCAR pit stop

In NASCAR, there are certain races you circle on your calendar. It goes without saying that the Daytona 500 and the Brickyard 400 at the Indianapolis Motor Speedway are two of these races. Even if you're not a racing fan, these are probably two races you've heard a great deal about. However, one race that often gets overlooked by the casual fan is the race at Darlington, South Carolina—the Southern 500.

It is a huge deal in our sport to win the Southern 500 because of the track's historical significance and the level of difficulty required to pull off the victory. The stifling South Carolina humidity, coupled with a worn-out racing surface, leads to a multitude of pit stops (north of ten), so you'd better bring your A game if you want to have a shot at winning. It's no wonder the track is nicknamed "The Track Too Tough to Tame."

It was on one particular hot and humid September night at the

Southern 500 that our driver was struggling with the handling of his car and "driving the wheels off of it," just to stay on the lead lap. Our crew chief knew that if we came into the pits for tires too early in the race, we would most certainly go a lap down, so he left our driver out on the track longer than all the other cars, hoping to catch a caution flag. The problem was, Darlington Speedway is notorious for chewing up tires, and every lap our crew chief delayed putting new tires on the race car resulted in seconds lost to our competitors on the track for lack of grip.

Once the crew chief finally called our driver onto pit road, it was too late. We had a great pit stop, but on exiting pit road, timing and scoring data rightfully dropped us several positions. It was *strategy*, not the pit stop, that lost us the spots, but the crew chief went off blaming the crew. We have often found ourselves on the business end of a verbal tirade from a crew chief in the middle of a race because of a miscommunication that led to a breakdown in execution. This time was no different. A lot of workplaces have scapegoats, and one of the most common for racing teams is the pit crew.

As the race progressed, we found ourselves in the exact same situation, only this time 165 laps later. We were not going to get blamed again, so we tried to make up for the seconds our crew chief had lost our team by pushing the pace. This turned out to be a display of reckless ambition and resulted in the fuel can getting dragged down pit road, still attached to the car, ultimately resulting in a penalty for equipment being removed from the pit stall. The crew chief's strategy might have been flawed, but we messed up in trying to prove him wrong. This negative starting place resulted in our efforts becoming hijacked by our mismanaged emotion.

People are routinely tangled up with resentment or bitterness. It's not all too uncommon for someone to say, "I'm going to prove him [or her] wrong." However, very rarely do you hear someone say, "I'm going to work hard today to prove him [or her] right."

When you try to prove people wrong, you allow emotion to cloud sound decision-making. Arrival mindset is how you arrive at work with the right mentality and attitude. Proving people right is how you maintain that attitude.

In our department, we do not want our athletes to prove people wrong. They are only allowed to *prove people right*. What we mean by proving people right is working hard—not only for ourselves, but also for all those people in our past and in the present: moms, mentors, family members, coaches, teachers, and bosses who have believed in us. People who sacrificed for us and poured their love into us simply because they believe in us. We have all had at least one person who believed in us or saw something good in us. Those are the people we should be trying to honor with how we live our lives.

We want our team to be positively motivated, not negatively motivated. The thing about proving people wrong is that, on the off chance that you do succeed, you're still bringing that negative experience into a space that you should be able to enjoy with those who have supported you. Bitterness gives people space in your head and your heart that they do not deserve. Pastor and author Steven Furtick once said that in the majority of these situations, the person you are trying to prove wrong is paying you no attention. *Zero*. You aren't on their radar, so leave them off yours.

Humanity Lost in Hierarchy

We once worked with a racing team that hired an executive director with lots of previous experience. He was basically third in the chain of command at the racing organization, and his start was a disaster. Among other things, he came right in, and, within weeks, had booted out a beloved woman from her long-time office who, for more than a decade, had served as the head of logistics.

The reason? He wanted an office with a window.

She never expressed it, but we could tell it bothered her and affected her level of trust and respect for her new boss. To lighten the mood, we told her she was welcome to move to our office, which we had affectionately labeled the "Temporary Contemporary." We, too, have had our office claimed by someone more important than us.

Windows are transparent allowing light in while keeping the elements out. Windows exist so that we can see and escape. We will be the first to admit that we all need to do a better job of seeing within and how our actions affect others. Our director could see outside, but couldn't see the aftermath of his decisions inside our reality.

As we increase the importance of relationships in the workplace, we first have to dismantle the hierarchical narrative that seems to dominate most workplace environments. Hierarchy is necessary to provide structure and a chain of command for operational effectiveness to thrive, but climbing the ladder at all cost is a dangerous journey. It can lead to dehumanizing others, turning them into stones to be stepped on along the way.

Most people exhaust themselves for days and years for a company, a team, or a brand. Why? What's the point of this? Is it to climb the ladder at all cost as individuals or lift each other up relationally as a team? Is it to work your way up a company so that you can one day have an office with a window or to uniquely impact others today—in the present?

Hierarchy is part of the makeup of any team or company, but with any title or promotion comes the chance for someone's ego to take over and begin to run the show. When conduct, demeanor, and decisions are purely ego-centric, it is difficult for people's humanity and dignity to be honored and validated. Ego, power, and control might make someone an executive or a boss, but it doesn't make that person a leader. Many organizations are led by managers who are not leaders. People's souls have gotten lost in the demand to perform, the hunger for power, and the execution of processes.

Bring It Back (Humanity)

When the tire changers hit the fifth and final lug nut, the jackman drops the jack for the car to launch back into the race. We teach our jackmen to *react to* the last lug nut hit, not *anticipate* it. A good reaction time is about two-tenths of a second. Occasionally, to save that two-tenths, the jackmen anticipate the drop and drop the car without the lug nuts being properly installed. It is then when those deflating three words come over the team radio: "Bring it back." The crew chief decides that the car must come back down pit road and be properly secured for the safety of the driver and best interests of the team.

For the best interests of your team, bring back the vehicle—*relationships*—that will move your company forward.

At the conclusion of every NASCAR season, we sit down and try to figure out ways in which we can make our pit crews more competitive. There is a minimal number of scenarios in which to create speed in a pit stop because the choreography of a pit stop remains rather static. NASCAR also mandates that we use track-issued air guns and air-pressure regulators, so advanced tooling also comes up short. The best avenue to quicken our pit stops often is to strengthen the relationships that bond our teams together. That is how you weaponize, or arm, your culture.

One thing we implemented early on with our team was a wilderness experience in the Appalachian Mountains of Tennessee. Mt. LeConte Lodge sits high atop the Smoky Mountains in Smoky Mountain National Park. Originally constructed in the 1920s, the lodge was built as a stopover for the Great Smoky Mountain Conservation Association. The value of Mt. LeConte for us lies in the fact that it is isolated from the rest of the world. There are no roads that can take you there. The only way to get there is to earn your way up there via a steep mountain climb. When you arrive, there is no electricity or natural gas, no cell phone service, and only two spouts with running water. Silence abounds.

Where this serves us well is that our crews are left with nothing to do but socially interact with each other. They don't have to manage distractions because there are none. What emerges is a clear picture of who works within the group and who resides outside it. With all the busyness stripped away, how we communicate and regard one another is on full display. Exercises and retreats like these position these crews to establish deep relationships and genuine connections.

Throughout the season, it is moving to see these deep relationships unfold. One time, our pit crew department was in the middle of a team meeting when one of our guys, from Brooklyn, New York, received an urgent call alerting him that his uncle had passed away. Without even leaving the meeting, the guy immediately burst into tears, right there in front of everyone. Most people—especially athletes like ours, who are often viewed as rough around the edges and macho—would internalize the pain and try to hold it together until after the meeting or when they were alone. But this man felt comfortable letting everything out, right then and there, because he knew he was in a safe place, surrounded by people who he knew had his back, not only as a teammate, but most importantly as a friend. He knew it was OK to not be OK around this group of people, who supported him both inside and outside the workplace.

This kind of relational safety and stability is something that each of us deeply wants. It speaks to our biology. We weren't made to be alone. The highest form of punishment, other than death, is isolation. But interestingly, most people go to work each and every day and feel alone, quarantined in an office or cubicle, sending out impersonal emails to coworkers just down the hall. Survival in the workplace often becomes all about self-preservation.

In Spartan culture, if a Spartan lost his helmet, breast plate, or spear in battle, he wasn't punished—those were the realities of war. However, if he lost his shield, he was severely punished, and often put to death, because losing one's shield affected the whole of the phalanx, letting the enemy in. It all goes back to protection. Connection was the key to survival.

We believe that a deep sense of togetherness can fill a hole in a company or team that money, power, and titles cannot fill. It can, over time, move a company forward more than resources can. As humans, we are in the pursuit of joy, not happiness. Money can bring you happiness, but it's teamwork and togetherness that bring you joy. We taste joy whenever we experience meaning and significance—a sense that we are tapping into a cause that is bigger than ourselves, a cause that is more about selflessly giving *of* oneself to others instead of selfishly gaining *for* oneself and using others.

So how do we create this kind of space?

Simply put, our space is based on belonging, not performance. We emphasize the importance of proving people right—inside and outside the workplace—more than we emphasize performance. We elevate relationships over results. We know that if our guys function as a cohesive unit and truly care for one another as people, the processes we employ to reach our goals will run more smoothly and efficiently.

A Deeper "Why"

If you're a coffee vendor and thinking about opening a new coffee shop, what's the purpose of the shop? Is it just another revenue stream? Another business opportunity? Is the coffee shop just a building? Or is it a place where people can come to connect with one another and dream up new ideas? A place for new missions to arise out of collaboration and help cure societal ills? A place for relationships to form and grow? A place for people around the city to come together and work alongside each other and know that they aren't alone?

If you run an insurance company, maybe you have the best, most unique products on the market, but what's the purpose behind these products? Were they developed for the mere sake of hoping to have a record-breaking financial year?

Or is the point of innovation—of moving forward—to really care for people and empower them to make better decisions about how they live their lives? To equip people with services that will help them feel less burdened and more secure?

When you really set out to prove people right, you help them tap into a deeper *why* of existence. You begin to see the communal, interconnectedness of everything instead of a life that is about accumulation and status. We can all quickly create a short list of five people who have profoundly impacted our lives, but can you quickly name five people whose list you are on?

A quick Google search of overall job satisfaction will show you studies from *Fortune* magazine, *US News & World Report*, *The New York Times*, and *CBS News* revealing that north of 40 percent of people feel isolated or lonely. In early 2018, the prime minister of Britain appointed a Minister of Loneliness to help address this "health epidemic" that is leading to increases in cancer, heart disease, depression, and suicide.[5]

We need to remember that our inherent desire for togetherness is a reflection of our biology—and yes, that includes in the workplace. We want to be protected. We want to be together. We are social creatures. Up until the last century, families always slept in the same room together. This provided security, stability, and community. Life might have been difficult, but people at least knew that they weren't alone.

For many in the United States, life has more opportunity than ever—professionally and financially—but people feel lonelier than they've ever felt. We're more connected than ever—through avenues like social media—but people feel more isolated than ever. Being overly concerned about our highlight reel has led to a lack of vulnerability and

---

[5] "PM Launches Government's First Loneliness Strategy," UK Government press release, last updated October 16, 2018, https://www.gov.uk/government/news/pm-launches-governments-first-loneliness-strategy.

increased comparison. And comparison is a thief of joy because it leads to either arrogance or hopelessness. Don't compare your documentary to others' commercials.

Workplace cultures break down whenever the health and stability of an environment hinge solely on performance or perception. When these are the driving factors and motivators for showing up at work each day, instability is birthed, and it is hard to move forward quickly on unstable ground. An environment of isolation instead of community rises from the despair of this instability. But, when we are fueled by the deepest meaning of our lives and connected to the people who believe in us, the engine of love and connection to one another propel us forward.

The people on our crews are more than teammates or employees. They are why our team matters. They are the deeper *why* of our workplace.

Belonging—The Modern Precursor to Performance

The centerpiece for factories during the Industrial Revolution was the assembly line, where an item would move down a conveyor belt, from worker to worker, each person performing a specific task…over and over…all day, every day. Though this increased productivity, work was monotonous and lacked individual creativity.

During this time, America went from an agrarian to an industrialized society, and the quality of life of lower-class factory workers in urbanized areas was mostly brutal. All the while, those in charge of the factories—the rich—became richer. To those sitting atop their ivory tower, their employees were nothing more than numbers. Humanity was stripped away in the name of productivity.

Production. Production. Production.

People were worth no more than the manual labor they provided and were just an end to a means.

This production-driven mindset that sparked the Industrial Revolution would go on to affect American education, too. Daily life at school was formulaic and regimented. Lines. Bells. Grades. Monotony. Performance. An overall coldness toward learning, just like it was toward working. But it made sense then. School, after all, was cognitively preparing children for the compliance, in factories or prison.

The Industrial Revolution was much-needed at that time in American history, increasing production, creating jobs, and erecting cities, but it seems that some of the effects of the Industrial Revolution are still plaguing America today. This cold, performance-focused, fear-inducing culture makes little sense now—in the classroom or the workplace. When this narrative is dominant, it leads to an overall lack of belonging. It is generally difficult for people to feel that they belong within an organization when they are easily replaceable. How can people feel like they belong if they are valued only for their time, not their ideas, opinions, or brilliance? There is a great meme on social media that says that if you died today, your job would be posted online before your obituary. When belonging is low, fear and anxiety are high.

Yet this is the dominant narrative in so many environments. How can people feel that they belong somewhere if they don't have a sense of pride for where they work? How can people feel like they belong somewhere if they feel like they have to walk on eggshells in the workplace or are overcome with a fear of failure because of their bosses' emphasis on performance? How can people feel like they belong if they are bored?

Most employees feel that a sense of safety and security is only attainable whenever their performance appeases their bosses. Yet this usually entails a career that feels more like a roller-coaster ride. Instead of being praised for their efforts, they are praised only for the results of their efforts, which often fluctuate.

We have tried to flip the script by assuring our guys that they are inherently part of the team and have a role to play, no matter their performance. We've never once yelled at them for their results. What we *have* come down on them for is any conduct or behavior that runs counter to our goals as a unit.

When it comes to their performance, one of our goals is to actually serve as a protective buffer between them and management. We absorb criticism but share praise. Any time there is a performance error on pit road, we are the ones who take the blame for the mistake. We take the responsibility as coaches, shifting the conversation toward how we could have done something better in practice that week or worked better with someone's fundamentals that week. Our guys already put enough pressure on themselves because of the meticulous, perfectionistic nature of our sport. They don't need to experience added pressure from their superiors that they ultimately know is already there.

Reframing the pressure to perform is vital for people's sense of belonging. We have all seen lives of superstar athletes or actors fall apart when the spotlight moves on from them. When people feel like their worth as a person hinges on their performance or the attention they receive, they will probably never feel like they belong. Because our guys know that they belong and that their coaches are in their corner, it facilitates an environment of trust, freedom, and individual contribution within departmental unison. They have a real sense of pride in their environment because they were the ones who created it.

From "I" to "Us"

Our first big decision, personnel-wise, as pit crew coaches was to decide who would become the starting jackman on our top car. The spot had been vacated by a veteran, and we had two talented jackmen competing for a starting spot. One was a veteran guy who had played in the NFL and was the organization's strength and conditioning coach. Another was a young kid whose only athletic experience was the varsity swim team in high school. However, the younger jackman worked incredibly hard and showed a lot of talent and leadership abilities. So instead of simply giving the position to the veteran, we decided to let them compete for the position.

Over the course of the off-season, the kid outperformed the veteran and won the spot. When the veteran was informed of the decision, he, in a fit of rage, stormed back to his desk, picked up a pen, and violently side-armed the pen at his computer screen. The pen cracked the screen, and the display spider-webbed. His monitor was broken.

Our first culture test as coaches was upon us. They say that in coaching, every tough decision you make is rewarded with the opportunity to make another tough decision.

Decision time:

- What behavior were we going to allow?
- How would we discipline him and not lose buy-in?
- How would our reaction affect the culture we were trying to create?

- How could we turn this into a teaching moment?

We sat down with the jackman and told him that we appreciated his drive to be the starter, but actions like that were no longer good enough for this department. We then told him that he needed to take his computer to the IT department, apologize to them for wasting their time with such a silly repair, and further, that he would take the entire department out to lunch as a way of apologizing for wasting their time.

Over the coming weeks, every member of the IT department, when seeing us, made a point of finding us to say, "Thank you. We've never had anyone do anything like that for us before."

The jackman understood the error of his actions and would go on to become a valuable member of our team and a wonderful teammate. He actually played a pivotal role in helping the future development of the young jackman, and people in some of the other positions, with their skills and fundamentals. All he needed was a little bit of redirection and inspiration to unleash his best self and become not only a better jackman, but most importantly, a better teammate. A leader.

This story demonstrates the paradigm shift in someone's mentality that is necessary to go from "proving people wrong" to "proving people right." He moved from being bitter and frustrated when his status was challenged to being supportive and relational, as he dedicated himself to others' progression on the team. In letting go of his ego, he was relieved from the notion that he had to focus solely on himself and his role. He began to press into all of us. He's a shining example of why getting from "I" to "us" is important. He not only continued to be a superb jackman but also became one of the better mentors we've coached. He is leaving a unique impact on our culture that stretches beyond his performance and will stretch long beyond his athletic career.

Relationships Fuel Communication and Accountability

Our guys enjoy being around each other so much that they take their families on vacations together. It's kind of ridiculous, actually. They'll have team workouts and all sorts of group activities.

But you know what they do while on vacation? They build and contribute to the overall group environment. They're completely removed from the workplace—completely removed from us or performance demands—yet they're having so much fun together that they're growing as a team, even while on vacation. At this point, the culture that has been created transcends the workplace, yet in transcending the workplace, it's the workplace that can benefit from the deep relationships that have been formed. Everything becomes integrated. People's lives become less compartmentalized. Communication and accountability naturally flow because that's what happens when genuine relationships and friendships are formed and left to flourish.

When you have a group of people all trying to prove one another right, it weeds out toxicity. When a team has this kind of core and supportive identity, anyone who comes in with an ego or begins to form an ego stands out. Communication and accountability are strengthened when each person is pulling the rope in the same direction. If someone begins to pull in a different direction, that individual is called out—not by the coaches, but by fellow teammates—and is encouraged to get back on the rope. That's when you know you've gained a competitive edge.

Oneness—unity—allows open communication and collaboration because the team is always aware of its collective identity: its culture.

Winning with Good People

With the right side of the car complete, everyone moves to the second phase of the pit stop. The front changer races to the left side of the car while switching his air gun back to the "off" position. The jackman drops the right side of the car while simultaneously moving toward the left side of the car. With the old right-rear tire in hand, the carrier heads to the old right-front tire. The rear changer hammers the fifth lug nut on the wheel stud as the car is dropped. The gasman extends his feet and body away from the gas can to prepare to disengage the first can. The driver shifts the car from neutral to first gear.

-The 5th second of a NASCAR pit stop

The standard hiring process for most companies is just that—standard. It usually involves carefully screening someone's résumé, LinkedIn profile, or Indeed portfolio, and, if impressed, moving into an interview with the potential hire. Those who have received a good education—or earned multiple degrees—have a chance of getting an interview. If they finished school with a good GPA, then they have a chance of getting an interview. If they have a lot of professional experience, then they have a chance of getting an interview.

The current state of our hiring process is a miss—and a giant miss at that. Financial guru Dave Ramsey is famous for saying that even a donkey can look like a thoroughbred for the first three interviews. Anyone can look good on paper. Anyone can say the right things for thirty minutes. What a résumé and interview do not reveal are the immeasurable gifts so vital to hiring high performers: emotional intelligence, grit, work ethic, integrity, and selflessness. Our goal is to unearth these traits in the hiring process before we ever spend our first minute of time or dollar of money in their development.

The first four chapters unpacked what we believe to be the necessary mindset and posture of individuals to make the workplace more meaningful and enjoyable (an inspired, healthy, and high-functioning environment and team). This chapter is about how to find those kinds of people. After all, trying to jam a puzzle piece into a spot that doesn't fit only damages other puzzle pieces and hurts the puzzle as a whole. There are lots of leaders in every industry trying to force puzzle pieces into a puzzle in which they do not belong.

But for those who know their direction but aren't gathering the right pieces, maybe it's because they aren't searching for the right traits in the hiring process. Or maybe it's because their hiring process wasn't thorough enough. No matter, the challenge and more efficient approach is to *find the right puzzle pieces*. But this takes patience and intention.

Trial Period

Years of hands-on training go into building a skill set that allows someone to pit a race car in 12 seconds. With that in mind, it is essential that we select the right people before we spend the next two years trying to get them up to speed. When we are thinking about hiring people, we challenge them with a carefully curated series of tasks aimed at getting past their "representative" in an attempt to get a glimpse at their true character. We bring them in on the most difficult day of the week, Wednesday, and evaluate them based on a series of checkmarks.

Wednesday is the most difficult because it's the most competitive day of practice and because of the intensity of the workout. "Awful" is often the word most of our veterans use to describe the Wednesday workout. It is a brutal, forty-five-minute slog that does everything in its power to chip away at your mental fortitude and turn you into a coward. This forces potential recruits to shed their "representative" and instead reveal to us what they are really about. We want to give them an opportunity to show us the depth of their work ethic, character, grit, and mental makeup. For us, Wednesdays act as a selection process, weeding out inflated egos, laziness, and selfishness on Day 1. We are excited to get new people, but if we act on that excitement and don't properly vet recruits, then it's our culture that takes a hit months later, when less-than-ideal traits are revealed. All it takes is one reckless hire to undermine everything that we—and our crews—have invested in our culture.

Your culture, after all, is only as strong as the lowest behavior that you tolerate.

When we bring a recruit in on Wednesday, the first thing we ask is that he show up at eight o'clock in the morning. This is when practice starts. If he shows up at eight, he has failed the first test. If he shows up at a quarter 'til, he moves on. If he shows up at seven, even better.

What we look for next is how engaged he is in his environment and the present moment. We want to see how he interacts with his teammates. We want to see if he gravitates toward some of the more menial work (for example, cleaning up dirty tires, wiping grease buildup off the tools, etc.). If he dives right in, unprompted, and is willing to perform some of the mundane day-to-day tasks, this communicates to us that he is present, aware, and finds value in doing the little things for his team. This earns him a checkmark.

Next comes the actual workout. We are not looking for him to lead the workout, move the most weight, or jump the highest. Instead, what we're looking for is work ethic and mental fortitude. These are the two most commonly shared traits among our most successful athletes, so we want to see those on full display on Day 1. We once had a guy who puked during the workout, but instead of quitting (which he had every right to do), he wiped his mouth with his shirt sleeve and pushed himself to the end of the workout. He was immediately dejected after the workout because he thought he had blown his opportunity. He believed that we were grading him on his performance and physical state and that stopping to throw up belied weakness. The reality, however, was just the opposite. We were looking for the deeper aspects of who he was—the kind of effort and resolve that would uniquely affect our department and move it forward. In the end, the guy who threw up but kept going is still going with us.

Next, we manufacture a scenario that will hopefully reveal the recruit's leadership abilities. Exhausted from the workout, we ask the recruit to get the attention of the other twenty-plus alphas on our team, have them put their hands in the middle atop one another, and inspire the group with an inspirational message. This sounds simple enough, but just imagine how daunting a task it would be to call up a group that includes former NFL players, Navy SEALs, and other highly accomplished collegiate athletes. Oh yeah, and it's your fourth hour on the job. If he can command the group with confidence and doesn't shrink in the moment, then he has the makings of a leader. His willingness to step up and lead—and his openness to doing something that might feel challenging or uncomfortable—will earn him the next checkmark.

Following the workout, we often ask a few of our guys to take the recruit out to lunch to get a feel for how he operates in a more casual setting. This is important because this will be the new normal if this recruit makes our team. We want an idea of the fit early on. Once our guys get back, we ask them about their honest opinion of the potential hire. We do this because we believe that those we coach have just as much ownership over our culture as we do. We also know that they'll be able to see things we might not be able to see. If we're satisfied with what they say about the recruit and the nature of their conversation, we give the recruit a fourth checkmark. It's only then, after receiving four checkmarks, that we move forward with hiring.

We recently had a recruit come in on a Wednesday who really demonstrated to us that he wanted to be here. He worked his butt off. He called the team together when we asked him. He was aware of the little things that needed to be done. He sailed through our vetting process. On paper, he didn't have a ton of experience, but he was a natural leader who was hungry to learn. His efforts were marked by passion and integrity. Sure enough, we would go on to find out from someone else that the recruit was living in a camper near our racing headquarters for as long as he needed to, until he earned a job in racing on a pit crew. He was willing to do whatever he had to do to be at the place he wanted to be.

It's not uncommon in our industry that has lots of turnover for us to hear prospects say things like, "I really need this job for my family." But we don't want guys who simply view being on our team as their job or career; we want people who feel a sense of calling in shaping an environment that is uniquely theirs. Each pit crew member can strengthen one another and has the ability to create impact beyond the X's and O's of pit stops.

We ended up hiring the guy who was living in a camper. It might have taken us two or twenty Wednesdays to find a recruit who was that passionate and dedicated, but we were patient. Our ultimate success is predicated on speed, but this is the one area where we are best served to slow down.

Sometimes people think we are foolish for taking so long to hire someone, to make changes, or for being so specific about who we hire, but the alternative is paying the salaries of employees who aren't making our company better. We don't know how you can simply say, "We don't have the time or money to manufacture a detailed experience in our hiring process" because once you hire someone, you are going to pour a ton of resources into that person's training and onboarding. Our investment on the front end is significant, but it has helped us build something that is sustainable.

Asking the Right Questions

Once a recruit has four checkmarks and both parties are interested in moving forward, we give that person a seven-page survey, which is an extension of the Wednesday workout. It's another opportunity for us to try to determine the depth of what that person is really about, but this time through how he responds to being challenged mentally. How does he think? What do his responses say about his story and journey? What do they say about what he has learned?

Here are some of the questions we might ask recruits in either an interview or a survey:

1. What do you want your legacy to be?
2. What are your non-negotiables?
3. What is the first thing you do when you fail?
4. What's the most important decision you have made in your life?
5. If you were offered a mulligan in life, what would you do over?
6. What were you put on this earth to do?
7. If you were to give an eighteen-year-old one specific piece of

advice, what would it be?
8. What's the smartest thing one of your teachers ever did?
9. What's the first thing you do in the morning?
10. What's the last thing you do before bed?
11. What difference did someone make in your life as a child?
12. If you were to rank all the people who have done this job in the past, tell me about number one and why you would put him/her there.
13. What do you think are the attributes that would make you a successful member of this team?
14. How do you plan to add to the strong culture that already exists here?
15. Who at your former place of work gave you the most energy and why?
16. Tell us in no more than two words what you think it is that we do.
17. What single project or task would you consider the most significant accomplishment in your career to date?
18. Tell us something that you believe in that almost nobody agrees with you on.
19. Tell us about a time when you almost gave up, how you felt about that, and what you did instead of giving up.
20. What makes you get out of bed in the morning?
21. What's your story? And, why does your story matter?
22. What reaction do people have when you walk into a room at work?
23. What are you most passionate about and how does that relate to this work opportunity?

None of these questions have to do with their skill set or past experience. None of these questions have to do specifically with racing. The purpose of each of these questions is to get past the "job interview" and see what it is that makes them who they are as people. Our questions are carefully crafted to avoid prepared responses and vanilla answers. We try to catch them off-guard in an attempt to get the authentic answer. We want to see people's depth and breadth of perspective. We know we have to get beyond their performance in pitting race cars if we want to catch a glimpse of what their unique contribution to our culture might be.

Emotional Intelligence > GPA + Skill

We recently heard that the hiring process at Lululemon—a high-end clothing chain that sells yoga and athletic wear—first entails a group interview and then a group workout of some sort. What's interesting about this process is that they are attempting to do the same thing we are doing, only in the sphere of retail: manufacture a scenario for a person's emotional intelligence (EI) to be exposed. We mentioned emotional intelligence earlier in this chapter but have yet to clearly define it. Let's dive into "EI" specifically in this section.

Psychology Today says that emotional intelligence is the "ability to identify and manage your own emotions and the emotions of others."[6] Leaders in companies are quickly learning that one's emotional intelligence is a more accurate precursor to success than both GPA and IQ. We want more than a skilled athlete. Lululemon wants more than someone who is polished in sales. Even though excelling in a workout has little to do with selling clothes, we would imagine that the hiring managers can see a lot about people's spirit, attitude, and teamwork through something as grueling as a workout, no matter their fitness level. For example, is the potential hire cutting corners in the workout or completing every step? If they are cutting corners, who's to say they wouldn't also cut corners in the store when in a stressful state? Does the potential hire try to support and help others when he or she is tired or struggling? If the prospect is concerned only about himself/herself, unaware of others' needs, would that person be a good teammate? How candidates manage their own emotions and the emotions of others is on full display during this tryout, and this is invaluable in evaluating whether or not a piece will fit in the puzzle of a culture.

Again, we believe hiring should be one of the more intensive and complex tasks for leaders. Most of the information on a person's résumé or portfolio says very little about a person's EI. A person can finish at the top of his or her class at an Ivy League school, but this doesn't

---

[6.] "What Is Emotional Intelligence?" *Psychology Today*, https://www.psychologytoday.com/us/basics/emotional-intelligence.

mean he or she is empathetic. It means that the person succeeded in the artificial environment of college. It speaks nothing about emotional intelligence or grit. However, what does speak volumes is a person who worked his or her butt off at two part-time jobs to get through community college. Isn't that the kind of person who should be hired? That's the kind of person who can lead, the kind of person who will pull weeds out of a company's environment and water it and inspire everything he or she touches along the way.

But will that person's résumé get through Human Resources?

Hiring people based on education and experience instead of empathy and emotional intelligence has led to a lack of diversity of thought and experience in the workplace. We will explore this topic more in the next chapter.

How the Right People Can Give Birth to a Bigger Purpose

Getting the right individual pieces on our team lets us know that we have individuals with perspective, character, and integrity. Putting those pieces together positions us to develop that same kind of depth collectively as a team, birthing within our culture a purpose that extends far beyond our performance on the racetrack.

In Jim Harbaugh's book, *Michigan Man*, he relates a story from his junior year as the quarterback at the University of Michigan. He recalls that he asked his quarterback coach, Jerry Hanlon, whether or not he thought that year's Wolverine team would be good or not. Hanlon said he didn't know.

Harbaugh was confused by the answer. Hanlon went on to explain that he would not know how good this football team would be for fifteen, twenty, twenty-five, or thirty years—that is when he would know if the guys he coached on that team would turn out to be good husbands, fathers, and stewards in the community, and that would dictate whether or not they had a good team that year. Hanlon wanted to win as badly as anyone, but he also saw his players as people who were so much more than what they did on the college football field.

A key denominator in a person's emotional intelligence is his or her empathy. Empathy gets a bad rap among leaders because most believe that being empathetic shows weakness. This could not be further from the truth. In fact, empathy is not the acceptance of poor performance but rather a deep understanding and connection to the human factors that drive performance. That's why one of the cornerstones to our group is volunteering. A person's level of empathy can say a lot about his or her perspective on life. That's why we also invite potential hires to participate in some of our nonwork-related service projects before hiring them. If they decide not to show up, falsely thinking that pitting race cars is the most important aspect to getting hired by us, that speaks volumes about their worldview and their perspective in life. We want people on our team who are well-rounded and have a personal mission in life that goes far beyond the paycheck they collect in racing.

One time, we had our entire group volunteer at a nearby, under-resourced elementary school to play with the kids at recess, take them healthy snacks, and, above all, simply spend time with them. When we got there, it was obvious to us who was taking the potential impact we could have on those kids seriously and who went just because it was mandated. Some of the guys were out on the playground, playing with the kids and making them laugh, whereas another group of guys was huddled around a soccer goal, simply talking among themselves. It said a lot about who our leaders were and who wanted to use their resources, time, and platform to help others.

In our guys' contracts, we are currently imploring management to offer them paid time off to volunteer. VTO, or Volunteer Time Off, allows them to pick the charity or cause of their choice and invest their time while getting paid by us. Beyond winning races, we want to leave a mark on our community. We used to organize and direct all the volunteer activities, but now it is something we are pushing the guys to originate themselves. Similar to the VTO where people have a mandatory eight hours that they have to volunteer somewhere during company hours, we want our guys to find something they are passionate about and build their own relationships with charitable organizations.

So many companies today just push forward at all costs. But if employees could just have an avenue to do something that truly feeds their souls, a company or team can begin to create a deeper-rooted identity. It's difficult for companies to find the value in volunteering because executives may think it takes up time and energy that could be used for work. They fail to see that volunteering inspires the soul of a person. But assembling the right pieces, armed with EI and kindness, will bring a collective perspective into the workplace that positively accelerates your culture and collaborative purpose. Brilliant strategy goes back to brilliant intention and planning, which rest squarely on motive. Positive motives such as hope and love tend to serve as better motivators over time, and they tap into the fullness of who we can be. The bigger purpose, then, is where what you *want* and what you *need* collide. It's the intersection of heart and mind, fire and desire. We call this "purpose-driven performance," and it's our mission to help everyone find this intersection.

Encounter

Our hiring process, the trial period, the surveys, and the empathy assessments are aimed at creating an environment of shared experiences and mutual interest. The "Principle of Least Interest" states that he or she who cares least hoards the most power in any group dynamic. Think of how different decision making would be for a woman with *all* her assets invested in a company versus a woman with only 1 percent invested. Simply, it's easy for the 1 percent to walk away or lack concern in important matters. We want people who are *all in*. The group suffers when one person consumes a majority of the energy, effort, or inspiration of its leaders.

During our first year as pit crew coaches, we oversaw four pit crews made up of a total of twenty-four athletes. The two guys who cared the least and put forth the least effort consumed 90 percent of our time. It seemed as though we were in an endless number of meetings with them, discussing their poor attitude, lack of respect, and tardiness. It was only in hindsight, after we had let them go, that we realized the error of our ways in not releasing them sooner. We are now hypervigilant to this fact and have vowed never to let it happen again.

We have settled on this, and you should consider the same: win with people who create a good experience. Think of the countless times you will pass a future coworker or teammate in the hallway, the countless conversations and communications, the meetings, and the pressure-packed moments. If the person you are working with creates a pleasant experience, your likelihood of a favorable outcome is likely. In healthy environments, people go out of their way to communicate, connect, encourage, and motivate teammates because they genuinely enjoy interacting with them.

We would love for you to wrestle with something before the next second of our pit stop with you: What happens when people interact with you?

Regardless of your profession, we want you to win and succeed, and that's going to take people. But not just anyone. It takes people who are aligned with a cause with meaning—people who create good encounters.

6

Diversity Isn't Just a Black or White Issue

The front changer plants his right leg preparing to dive into the left-front wheel. The jackman, with his 25-pound jack, strides past the front-center (nose) of the car. The carrier angles both used right-side tires toward the wall. The rear changer goes from a kneeling position to a lateral sprint toward the left side of the race car. The gasman throws the first fuel can over the wall to a fuel catcher while eyeing the second can.

-The 6th second of a NASCAR pit stop

Why does the talk of diversity make us so uneasy? And why, when someone talks about diversity, do we immediately default to hiring quotas and think of the number of black employees we have compared to the number of white employees? The ratio of black to white employees has very little to do with diversity.

Confused? Let us reframe it in terms of cars.

Imagine you won the lottery, and your dream of becoming a car collector could finally become a reality. You take your newfound wealth to the local Ford dealership, and there you spot a dozen brand-new Ford Mustangs. Giddy with excitement, you want them all. There are seven "midnight black" ones and five "pearl white" ones. So you buy them all and showcase the fleet in your garage. You invite a noted car collector over to the house to unveil your new collection. The collector's initial reaction? Obviously unimpressed in seeing that you bought twelve of the same car. Having seven black mustangs and five white mustangs does not make your car collection diverse. It's the same car! The same engine, the same transmission, the same interior, the same upgrades, the same everything. The fact that everything underneath the paint is the same lends itself to similarity rather than diversity.

Most seem to think that color is what makes an environment diverse. This is sometimes the case; diversity of color often brings people together who are very different in their thinking, experience, and backgrounds, but it is not always the case.

For example, we recently talked with an executive who works at one of the leading tech companies in Silicon Valley, a company long thought of as a leader in diverse work spaces. He related to us that, "We have a really diverse group, but we had one guy who recently quit." He continued, "He was a staunch conservative, and I guess we ran him out."

So in this context, what does diversity mean? The executive might have believed he had a diverse team because he had a few black people, a few Indians, a few white people, a good mix of men and women, and a couple of people in the LGBTQ community. But if every single person on the executive's team is a liberal—so much so that it felt oppressive to the one conservative—is the team really that diverse in its thinking?

Twelve Mustangs.

If every single hire went to an Ivy League school, is that team diverse in its experience? If all employees are Millennials, are they diverse in age? If all of them are high-energy and extroverted, are they diverse in their personalities?

Don't misunderstand us here. By harping on the lack of diversity in the Mustangs, we're not advocating for color-blindness, either. We long for a day when all parties involved believe that "We're all the same as Americans." Yet, as an African American and Canadian writing this book, it can be frustrating to hear someone say, "I don't see color" or "The only culture that matters is the American culture." These kinds of statements neglect the real experiences and backgrounds that people have due to their skin's story or heritage. To dismiss culture is to dismiss identity, and we are not advocating that. Cultures make people who they are.

What's your "skin story's" past? Whatever tone you represent, the past has little to nothing to do with your redefining that story moving forward. The body consists of organs, the largest being skin, which makes up about 15 percent of your body weight. Skin is made of three layers, with the epidermis being the smallest of the three. Of that smallest layer, less than 15 percent includes melanocytes (the layer that includes pigmentation). Let's distill skin color for a second: Why are we so quick to make judgments based on a visual prompt that speaks to roughly 1 percent of who a person truly is?

So, then, what is true diversity?

We don't think most people have the wrong definition of diversity. Considering our country's history, many people's definitions are a step in the right direction. Most definitions, however, are still incomplete. We believe diversity can be taken even deeper. So we have developed the acronym TEAM as a framework for people to apply to their workplace however they see fit. TEAM stands for thought, experience, age, and motor.

Diversity of thought is true variety of opinion—where there are people who are on polar opposite sides ideologically, whether that be political, spiritual, or social. Diversity of experience is true variety of background—where there are people who come from different socioeconomic, educational, and family situations. Diversity of age can mean the obvious—people who are both young and old—but can also refer to the length of time someone has been in a particular industry. A lot of times, companies become stagnant or set in their ways, and therefore unable to evolve, when they are prejudiced toward young people or newcomers with fresh ideas. And finally, diversity of motor is true variety of personality—where they are people who are both introverted and extroverted, both emotional and calm, both quiet and outspoken, etc.

Lack of diversity is fueled by fear and comfort. Fortune and brilliance, however, favor the courageous. Executives and bosses tend to hire out of a space of familiarity: people they already know, like family or friends or previous coworkers, people who look like them, or people who resemble the skill sets of others who have held similar positions in the past. Filling the parking lot with twelve different-colored Mustangs becomes a facade that masks the fear of true diversity. The different colors are good, but we also want more than Mustangs. We want trucks and bikes and SUVs. Diversity has the potential to divide people, but if you are willing to attempt to understand it and learn from it, it can bring people together and be a powerful ally. If we can unite beyond the fear, we have an opportunity to be brilliant.

Diversity of Thought

Not to get too political, but for the sake of a good illustration, picture President Donald Trump's cabinet as opposed to Senator John McCain's funeral. Trump's cabinet is composed of people who mostly look the same, and his appointments to these positions are based on loyalty—a loyalty that seems to hinge on whether or not they support his ideas.

At McCain's funeral, however, three eulogists spoke. All had experienced considerable strife and conflict with McCain ideologically: President Barack Obama, who beat him in the 2008 presidential election; Vice President and long-time Senator Joe Biden, who disagreed with McCain often in Congress; and President George W. Bush, who beat McCain in the 2000 Republican primaries. All three of these people were the exact opposite of "loyal" in the way that Trump might define it because they were all so different in their thinking. Yet these were the people who McCain wanted to speak at his funeral. It seems that the commitment of McCain, Obama, Biden, and Bush to the American people and to public service created a unity among them. Their diversity of thinking flourished and made them stronger, even amid disagreement, tension, and frustration.

Diversity of thought cannot be cultivated in self-constructed echo chambers. Yet echo chambers are usually what are constructed whenever higher-ups emphasize loyalty and quench creativity and diversity by manufacturing fear or instability in the minds of those below them. Many in the workplace have fragile egos that cannot handle people thinking differently than them. They simply want others around them to support their own ideas. So they surround themselves with "yes men" and "yes women" so they do not have to listen or learn from anyone else in the workplace. This is the exact opposite of diversity of thought.

In our interview and survey questions in the previous chapter, you might remember this prompt: "Tell us something that is true that almost nobody agrees with you on." We intentionally crafted this prompt to attract and cultivate diversity of thought. For example, we recently had a guy answer the question by telling us that he was an ardent Trump supporter. We asked him why, and he gave us a number of intelligent and passionate explanations. Though neither of us necessarily agreed with his position, this man's support of Trump didn't make us respect him less. We actually admired him all the more for standing up for something he believed in and for being passionate about it. We hired him.

On a holistic level, we try to approach each day with the mindset that each person on our team—ourselves included—owns an equal percentage of the pie that makes up our culture. We have twenty-one athletes in our program, and regardless of whether they are ten-year veterans or first-year guys, their voice carries with it $1/21^{st}$ amount of the weight in decision making and opinion.

A great majority of employees in the workplace don't feel comfortable sharing their thoughts, concerns, or ideas because they feel like they have little ownership over the team's direction. When bosses bark orders down the chain of command all the time, how can you feel like you have any say in the company or team's direction? We believe we can tap into this diversity of thought by honoring each person's equal ownership of and contribution to the culture. When you can help someone to feel valued and accepted, you can begin to tap into his or her depth as a person. When you inspire people to share that depth with their teammates, diversity of thought flourishes.

Diversity of Experience

One of the roadblocks to employers honoring diversity of experience is tradition. This is how cycles perpetuate themselves and why teams are often built from the same kind of people for years. In these instances, nostalgia acts as a disease that births dangerous statements like, "We have always done it this way."

For example, early in our racing career, we were working with a team that needed to hire someone to be the Director of Sponsorships, the person who basically manages relationships with all the team's racing sponsors. We suggested that they hire someone internally and recommended a woman who had helped us with a number of initiatives over the years. She was more than qualified and was great with people. She was a perfect fit for the job and was passionate about the position. She wasn't just qualified; she was a superstar. The only issue? The Director of Sponsorships had always been a male.

Those who were making this hire might not have directly said this, but their hesitancy was obvious. They already had a picture in their mind of what the Director of Sponsorships would look like based on what they had seen in the past.

A lot of times, judgments and prejudices like this unfold on a subconscious level. People's names are removed from consideration for a position without any explanation at all. NASCAR is an industry born in the South and is governed by men of legacy and immense wealth. The two groups that are discriminated against the most are women and people of color. In her book *I'm Still Here: Black Dignity in a World Made for Whiteness*, Austin Channing Brown discusses how her parents gave her a first name that would fool universities and future employers into thinking that she was a white man instead of a black woman so she might increase the likelihood of getting opportunities.

It's important for people who are in a position to make hires, or who build teams, to be aware of these potential prejudices that can unfold even on a subconscious level. When the executives at the racing team we worked for didn't bring the woman who we recommended in for an interview, we thought, *Maybe this is why this position always seems to be vacant every couple of years: because you keep hiring the same type of person who has the same kind of experience.* This woman was soon offered a job doing similar work with one of the top NFL franchises but with a much larger budget, platform, and title. She accepted the job. Great for her, but a missed opportunity for excellence on the race team.

As discussed, diversity of experience is often lacking in companies and teams today because of the emphasis that has been placed on performance and educational pedigree when weeding out résumés of potential employees. As we talked about in the last chapter, a person's past professional experience and the college he or she attended cannot possibly give employers a full picture of that person's emotional intelligence, integrity, and work ethic. We have a feeling that there are a lot of people out there who could have radically changed the trajectory of a company or team but were eliminated early in the hiring process just because someone else received a better education and therefore got their résumé past the front lines of Human Resources. Again, diversity of thought, experience, age, and motors is all about the depth of the person. Employers can't see a person's depth if they eliminate people in the hiring process based on surface criteria.

People are right to consider race, gender, and sexuality in their definitions of diversity because often, there are socioeconomic influences and stereotypes at play in the hiring process. But there is a danger when the definition of diversity becomes all about image.

We once heard a story about a team manager at one of NASCAR's major teams at the time who had a meeting with a potential sponsor who was interested in funding the team at a primary level (north of $10 million). The battle for sponsorship dollars is fierce, so when an opportunity presents itself, there is no room for error. But this particular meeting was over before it started. As the potential sponsors walked into the conference room, the team owner shook the titular CEO's hand, skipped over the actual CEO (the wife), and then shook the vice president's hand. *Ten million dollars down the drain.* Just like that. The team manager falsely assumed who the CEO might be based on his past experiences in the industry and his unconscious biases. His ignorance led to an action that turned out to be highly offensive. His thinking that people in leadership must look like him indicated a blindness to diversity.

If you walked down pit road on any given Sunday, you would find that our pit crew looks quite different from other pit crews. This was unintentional regarding race yet very intentional in validating—and seeing the strengths and gifts—in people who have a wide range of backgrounds and experiences. A lot of times, this does result in a culturally and racially diverse group because experiences vary drastically across different races and cultures. This has been to our benefit and has helped us navigate a number of issues.

One issue we have had to confront in NASCAR is kneeling during the national anthem as a form of nonviolently protesting police brutality. President Trump has publicly praised NASCAR for its patriotism and condemned the NFL. A number of racing team owners have even spoken out and said that they would fire employees who protested during the national anthem. But this issue became especially personal for our group in 2016 when Keith Lamont Scott was killed by Charlotte law enforcement. Having the most racially diverse pit crew that year, the issue was not something that could simply be ignored, especially once Charlotte was at the center of the conversation.

Many of the white guys on our team that year had the stereotypical background that you might expect someone who is interested in NASCAR to have; they did not have a connection to the reasons behind the protests in Charlotte or why their black teammates would have any desire to kneel during the national anthem. Simply put, most found kneeling during the anthem to be offensive to the military and veterans. On the contrary, most, if not all, of our black guys had grown up having a complicated, conflict-filled relationship with law enforcement, and many had personally experienced racial profiling by policemen.

Leaving Red Bull Racing one evening, I (Metcalf) was pulled over for what I thought was a routine traffic stop. That narrative quickly dissipated as multiple law enforcement cars stopped traffic on both sides of the road and drew their weapons. Unfortunately for me that day, I was driving a gold Lexus (that I had bought and paid for) on a day that a silver Lexus had been reported stolen by a black man. I was targeted because there is not an overabundance of black people driving around in Lexuses in the small town of Mooresville, just north of Charlotte, so I fit the description. I'll never forget seeing my life flash before my eyes as I saw an officer in my mirror, inches away, pointing a gun at me—an event that paralleled the vapor of moments before the end of Keith Lamont Scott's life. The police tore through everything in my car once I was removed from it. They never apologized. They said it was protocol. I cried on my way home and still do when I see others unsuccessfully navigate that thinness between life and death. Like tiptoeing on a razor blade, it was uncomfortable. It hurt me emotionally, but at least I was alive.

So, as Charlotte was the center of a national conversation and tensions were high, we gathered everyone together and started a conversation to bring awareness to both "sides" of the argument. We've learned over the past decade that people don't need to "win" those arguments

—they just need to feel heard, and it's up to leaders to create space for carefully moderated conversation. Sharing stories is usually the best way to help someone else see another perspective.

There was tension and conflict, as well as a number of ignorant things that were said, but our black guys were patient with our white guys. Our black guys learned that not all white people have stereotypes. Some are apathetic, not because of hate or fear, but simply from being unaware. We think that even in the moments when there were misunderstandings or tempers flaring up, each of our guys knew their teammates appreciated them.

At the start of the next season (2017), one of our black guys stood up in a preseason meeting and confidently said, "For any of the old guys or new guys that just joined the team, a lot of people tiptoe around the black/white thing. But if any of you ever have any questions, I don't care what it is, just ask me; we'll talk." This is the kind of conversation and healing that can unfold whenever people realize that their backgrounds and experiences are strengths that can be offered as gifts to others. These conversations benefited us as a team and helped us perform on race day in a unified state during a divisive time, having sifted through tension and conflict together. But most importantly, these conversations informed us of experiences, uncovered perspectives, and opened the door for deeper connections.

Diversity of Age

In chapter 4, we told the story about the veteran jackman who lost his position to a young developmental kid, having gotten beat out in a tryout. At first, the veteran lost his cool and chucked a pen through his computer screen, but once he was calm and could catch the vision of the culture and our direction as a team, he went on to become a mentor and great teammate.

Though diversity of age is pretty self-explanatory, this story is a good example of how it's easy for the ego to become inflated after doing something for a long time. Most brand-new cars need to be broken in before they hit peak performance, but some are ready right off the floor. But typically, no matter the make or model, a time comes when the performance drops off and change is necessary. Pruning is necessary; the environment depends on it. Otherwise, nutrients are wasted on dying branches.

The more of an "expert" you become, the more difficult it can be to respect the opinions of others, especially newcomers or young people. But often, these are the people who can bring a fresh perspective and contagious energy to a team. Those who are less experienced are not always limited the way a more tenured employee can be. Veterans sometimes view problems that arise through a lens of limitation because they have had experiences that don't go as planned, so they become more cautious in their approach. Someone with less experience views the exact same problem through a lens of possibility, and that's incredibly powerful. We welcome the opinions of the newest members of our team because they are seeing our processes and our culture with "new eyes." Their honest feedback has more than once proved to increase the horsepower of our group. Our oldest tire changer is forty-two, our youngest is twenty-three, and they are friends. Theirs are the first two opinions we seek when we assess tire-changing protocols. The range of these conversations is invaluable.

Conversely, those who are new to a job also need to understand that there is much wisdom to be gained from those who have been in a specific environment for a while, but they should also feel comfortable to express their ideas. Though Millennials get a bad reputation in the workplace for failing to hold on to a steady job for more than a couple of years or for lacking the eagerness to go the extra mile, one thing they are doing is bringing some emotional intelligence and accountability into the workplace. We know of many Millennials who have an insatiable desire for something more—to make an impact in the world through their work. They identify with purpose over titles. They do not just work their way toward retirement but rather toward finding a vocation that ignites their passion. Our parents worked very hard to make a living for themselves and give us opportunities that they did not have as children. However, that has created the first American generation that has grown up comfortable, not quite having to bear the burden or responsibility that shaped our preceding generations.

According to multiple researchers, the brain has two primary functions: to survive/thrive and to conserve calories. This dates back to the years before air conditioning and heat, grocery stores, cars, insulated houses, and the internet—back to when nothing was comfortable about humanity. Unless inspired otherwise, our brains tend to inform us to do nothing or be on cruise control, to wait for the moment for the comfort to be taken away before taking any daring action. The quickest way to get someone off cruise control is to create traffic ahead of them. If you want to inspire Millennials, accelerate and decelerate responsibility at times; create specific challenges for them beyond just performance; inspire them to be the best version of themselves; and encourage them to be on the lookout for opportunities that may better align with their personal core values. Last, if you embrace that they may not be long term-employees whom you "own," they might actually stick around for a while.

The pie-style approach of leadership, where each team member owns an equal portion of the culture, can be especially empowering to young people or newcomers. They are often the ones who feel that they have little to offer a workplace environment because of their inexperience. This equal ownership and responsibility over our culture keeps people of all ages humble and open to new ideas.

Diversity of Motors

What if your proverbial parking lot had a Ford Power Stroke F-250 diesel pickup truck, a vehicle that was completely powered by solar energy, a Chevy Volt, a Freightliner tractor trailer, a panhead Harley Davidson, a Chevrolet Suburban, a Ford GT, a Toyota Camry, and a minivan to accompany a few Mustangs? Would you be as concerned as the person who owned only twelve Mustangs if there were a major shortage in fuel or a section of road where a group had to pull another or a stretch where the terrain was rocky? Probably not.

The ability to pivot amid fast-changing trends and navigate uncharted market space is often directly correlated to the different motors within your team. Our group consists of people who are pessimists, optimists, raging liberals, staunch conservatives, early birds, night owls, class clowns, nerds, Yankees, and hillbillies; people who barely made it out of high school to college dean's-listers to an Ivy League graduate; people who are quiet, brash, measured, loud, talkative, contemplative, confident, and meek.

Uniformity is not a requirement for unity. But assembling the right motors makes unity a possibility.

Motor is everything—not just on race day, but for your environment as well. There have been a number of times during our years as coaches when we have traded personality for skill. We have cut talent to make room for someone who has more passion or has tapped more into his or her own depth as a person. It's obvious when someone has a big motor because there is a clear passion behind that person's efforts. We want people who are intrinsically motivated, people who move our culture forward, and never drift into stagnancy or complacency. These people have the innate ability to lift the group up as a whole.

This passion—a strong motor—however, can be delivered through all kinds of personalities. This is another area where it's easy for employers to carry stigmas into the hiring process. A shy, quiet, or seemingly awkward person could turn out to be incredible at fostering one-on-one relationships with sponsors. An extrovert with charisma could turn out to be a terrible leader, like a guy we mistakenly hired early in our careers without careful evaluation of his character. A Type A perfectionist could help improve the minute details of a pit stop. And a person with an easygoing, laid-back personality could help the team members not take themselves too seriously and dissipate the pressure of intense moments. Passion can reveal itself in a plethora of ways through the uniqueness of an individual. Early birds can get in before the sun awakens and set up, while the owls can stay behind and break everything down. Both are needed. Both can feel competent and authentic about who they are, what they do, and how they contribute. Passion can reveal itself in a plethora of ways through the uniqueness of an individual, and our job is to keep passion flowing at all times. We have a body of work to do, split up based on responsibilities, roles, talents, and goals. Sometimes it's early, sometimes it's late, but when the work is done, we go home.

The challenge as an employer is to refrain from bringing preconceived notions into the hiring process about what you think someone's personality should look like. That's the equivalent of showing up to a golf course with a bag full of drivers.

Leaders let their culture down whenever they aren't diligently working to intentionally arm the team with diversity and seeking to develop each person's gifts on that team. They let their culture down whenever they write someone off just because he or she isn't what the leader expected them to be. Manufacture a space during the hiring process for a person's passion to shine or lack of passion to be exposed, but then be open to how that passion is delivered through the uniqueness of that human being's personality.

Each person has gifts that you, as a leader, have the opportunity to discover, unleash, and multiply. If times are good, bad, or ugly, you'll have someone who can thrive, lead, and inspire. Going back to the introduction, we dream of creating strong, powerful cultures. So we ask this question: Can you create more force in punching with a finger or a fist? In the words of Booker T. Washington, "We can be as separate as the fingers, yet one as the hand in all things essential to mutual progress."

Diversity is wholeness. A wholeness that allows us to walk in the shoes of others, that overpowers hatred or division, and that increases perspective. We desperately need each other. We need diversity.

7

Creating Environment

The front-tire changer strikes lug nut two of five off the car. The jackman, skipping over the front tire changer's air hose, locates a small piece of tape signaling the position of where the jack needs to be inserted to lift the left side. The carrier either carries or rolls both used tires past the nose of the car while looking for the spoke of the new left-front tire. The rear changer also switches the gun to the "off" position, preparing to slide into the left side of the car. The gasman grabs the second fuel can from behind the wall while once again locating the fuel coupler.

-The 7th second of a NASCAR pit stop

Imagine sketching out a company on a piece of paper. Whether it's big or small, you would definitely draw three things: people, processes, and precedents. These three elements constitute environment.

People are necessary to work for the company to execute collective "choices." Processes are needed for efficient production within the company and guiding choices. And precedent informs choices based on past data and successes/failures.

Without these, you don't have a company. Even if it's a one-person company, these three are necessary.

No matter where you are in the hierarchical structure of your company, you can be a leader and uniquely impact culture, thus moving the environment forward. Your greatest opportunity as a leader is to positively influence this movement. Culture distilled boils down to the daily choices you make within a given environment over time. You're a culture creator.

Sheep, Lions, and Fleas

An Arabic proverb says, "An army of sheep led by a lion would defeat an army of lions led by a sheep."

Currently, many environments and cultures have sheep at the helm. Sheep have simple routines. They are rarely independent-thinking. They're not assertive. You could say they're insecure, needy even. And they require daily interaction. If you take a sheep down a path to get water five days in a row but are busy on the sixth day, that sheep is going to get dehydrated or annoyingly ask you to show her where the water is…again. A sheep doesn't lead; it needs a leader and direction. Lions, however, are fearless, protective, and bold. They are called kings, and deservingly so.

Many people in management around the country are lions but are caged. They're talented and strong. They have vision, power, and capacity. Yet they're floundering because someone who is supposed to be leading them isn't interested in their development, only their output. They don't know which way to attack because the sheep above them elevate process over people and are focused on their own routines.

When distilling big matters, we like to think small. The flea is a tiny insect with a compelling story. Fleas don't have wings, so they cannot fly, but they can jump incredibly high for their size and glide long distances. Multiple experiments have been conducted in which fleas have been placed in glasses they can easily jump out of. Researchers will then place a lid on the jar, and over time, the flea will jump just high enough to not hit its head on the "ceiling." Once that height is set, the lid can be removed, and the flea will never make it out of the glass jar again. The flea is created to soar but never will.

Do you relate more to the sheep, the lion, or the flea? We often talk to Millennials who lack direction and feel "lost" in their careers and jobs, managers who feel stunted in their development, or leaders who are so buried in process that they have no time to actually lead the people under them.

Creating a healthy environment isn't just about maximizing people's talents; it's about unleashing their gifts and getting them out of the jar instead of keeping them in it. This is why good leadership matters. To be honest, this is the reason why we are writing this book. We are passionate about building people and leaders, but we have been instructed repeatedly to "focus on pit stops." There is a good chance we will be asked to leave when this book is released, but we live by the motto that fortune favors the brave: we would rather risk the uncertainties of lionhood than shrink to the comforts of the jar. Leading requires intellectual and emotional fortitude. It starts with one bold, daring person who will have courage. No one can determine who you will become—that is up to you.

Leading starts with lions. It starts with you.

Owners vs. Renters

When we decided to become pit coaches, we inherited a program that came with significant challenges. Upon our arrival, we found out that our predecessor had sold most of the equipment out the back door, that the company had not protected our two best athletes (who had subsequently left and signed with another race team), and that our current roster was largely bereft of talent. To compound that, we had significantly less money than other teams to attract and sign talent. And when we say significantly less, we mean we had about half the budget of the big teams to assemble a group that could be competitive on Sundays.

We made a decision early on that if we were to have any chance of competing with the big teams, we had to have guys who were invested in the program. Guys who were all in. Guys who were so committed to Plan A that they didn't even operate with a Plan B.

We identify these types of guys as *owners* based on a concept from Elevation Church in Charlotte. How does Elevation mobilize thousands of people to selflessly volunteer to serve their communities? *It attracts owners.* There's a reason why it's one of the fastest-growing churches in the country. Whereas all churches, teams, and organizations are filled with *people*, not all are filled with *owners*.

If you are renting a house or apartment and a pipe bursts, what do you do? Without hesitation, you call your landlord. But let's say you are the owner of a condo or a house and a pipe bursts. Then what do you do? You have to fix it yourself or pay someone to fix it. As an owner, it hurts when something breaks—when something goes wrong—because you are the one who has to take care of it. But there is also more reward on the back end, whether that is paying off your mortgage one day or selling the house for more than you paid for it. It's the power of pride.

A renter isn't going to spend his own money making major improvements to a residence. He isn't going to add a porch or build onto the house. But an owner might *add* a porch, *build* onto the house, *knock* down walls, or *change* fixtures. Owners have more responsibility but also experience more fulfillment—something we are all looking for.

Part of creating a healthy environment is helping people feel a sense of ownership in the space where they work. Owners want to fix problems. Owners go out of their way to make improvements to products and processes that will move the company forward. When people feel at home, they'll treat it like a home. Owners aren't just working for a paycheck. Owners aren't just working to get through the week. They see the potential short-term and long-term benefits of investing all of themselves in their home.

According to speaker and author Andy Stanley of North Point Community Church in Alpharetta, Georgia, leaders who don't listen will eventually be surrounded by people who have nothing to say. Every voice matters. We want unity, not uniformity. Each person's equal ownership of our culture is what inspires our oneness and that starts with each person sharing his or her concerns, ideas, and differences with the group. And we try to replicate this same pie-style approach on race day. As we've mentioned, in a five-person pit crew, each person owns a *fifth* of the group. There's enough pressure in our sport already. We want the individual members of our crew to take ownership of their actions, mindset, and emotions, not fearing what will happen if they don't perform.

A small but important example of this was the locker assignment at practice. What we noticed during our first week as coaches was that only the starting pit crew members had lockers. Some even had their equipment taking up two lockers. None of the backup guys had lockers. Instead, they had to haul their gear out to practice every day. We didn't like the precedent this set, so we had the lockers immediately replaced with about thirty cubbies of equal size. This demonstrated that each person's contribution to the pit crew department carried equal weight. Each had different roles to play within the culture, but we need each person's gifts to move our culture forward.

To create a culture of owners, however, requires a tough ask. Instead of renting your house, would you consider selling it? Renting a house perpetuates renters. Selling a house creates homeowners. Think about that. If you want owners, you'll have to give up some control, a.k.a. ownership.

We were fortunate to have a very forward-thinking crew chief during our time at MWR. Coincidentally, it was also the time we both personally experienced unparalleled success on pit road and the track. We won several races over two seasons, and we were a top-five pit crew both years. On the very first race of the season in Year 1, we gathered in the hauler for what would be the shortest and only pre-race meeting of the year. Our crew chief simply said to the crew, "You guys know what you are doing. Just go out do your job and execute. Thanks!" All it took was 12 seconds for him to give us the freedom to be excellent.

We often have drill days when we let the guys decide what they want to work on. They often work on things that we as coaches would not have previously identified, but these days are always productive because the guys have initiated ownership in their own development. They take the house to places we cannot on our own.

Communicating Expectations

No matter the sport, a big team meeting is usually held at the start of the season. The vision for the season is established. Principles are laid out. Expectations are communicated. In football, a team could be coming off a Super Bowl victory the season before, but the meeting is still going to happen the next season. A team could have lost every game the season before, but the meeting is still going to happen. Our pit crew department also starts each season with an "expectations meeting." Can you imagine a beginning-of-the-season meeting not happening in sports? Where players just show up on the first day of training camp or spring training, or whatever it may be, and just do whatever they think they're supposed to do?

Yet this is what happens much of the time in the business world. At the turn of the calendar year, fiscal year, or turn of a financial quarter, most people just show back up at work and keep doing the same thing they were doing before. And when there is a change in personnel or someone gets hired, they just get thrown into the existing flow and are expected to join along after a brief onboarding procedure. Culture gets lost when there is a lack of evolution. It's usually not until there is a crisis, a grand idea, or a corporate shift that a meeting is called to communicate new expectations. Business has a lot to learn from athletics when it comes to establishing vision and direction.

The best expectation meetings we've had in racing are the ones that are collaborative—when it's each person on the team contributing to the vision and mission that is being established. We develop the direction that we want to go…together. Maybe that's through crafting a mission statement together or brainstorming our principles for the year and writing them on a whiteboard. Open participation breeds ownership.

Healthy environments have leaders who establish expectations and constantly revisit them throughout the year. Communicating expectations establishes clarity and direction. It helps people understand what they should be doing and what they shouldn't be doing. When clear expectations aren't established, a company looks a lot like a sheep leading a pack of lions. There is so much power and potential in the pack, but it is unclear where they are supposed to go or what they are supposed to do.

Wiffle Ball, Knockout, and the "Canada Day Classic"

One of the key lessons we took away from our experience as pit crew members at Red Bull, our first stop in our journeys in racing, was how fun work could be. We learned that pitting race cars didn't have to be the cold, performance-driven, cutthroat, high-pressure environment that so many of our colleagues experienced at other racing teams. There were countless days when we each drove to work in the morning laughing in the car because of something that happened the day before. Rarely do you hear people say, "I can't wait to go to work," but that was exactly how we felt. Every. Single. Day.

Days at Red Bull Racing were made enjoyable through an intentional mix of competition and tormenting one another with odd pranks. One mechanic went so far as to hook one guy's horn in his truck to his brake pedal so that on his drive home, every time he hit the brake pedal, his horn would blare. Needless to say, the drivers in front of him on his drive home were less than impressed. This was the type of camaraderie you would often find in a football or hockey locker room. The pit crew building at Red Bull Racing had an intercom system, and people would get in early to run the intercom. Why? Because jokes started flying the second we walked through the door.

If you had pulled into the Red Bull Racing parking lot on any given day and saw the unmistakable enjoyment and fun we were having, you probably wouldn't have thought that we knew anything about excellence or success. Anyone outside of Red Bull Racing would have probably thought they were pulling into a circus. But the truth is that we had two outstanding pit crews and even won the 2008 World Pit Crew Championship. We experienced the highs and lows of every young team our first few years. But by the third year…let's just say our contracts went from being performance-heavy with bonuses for every fast pit stop to strictly salary. No one blamed them; we would have been paid way too much. Of twelve top-level guys, more than half were offered jobs from the big NASCAR teams, which included big raises—but no one left Red Bull. Money can get you many things, but it doesn't buy environment.

Everything at Red Bull Racing was a competition, whether it was playing wiffle ball or hockey in the parking lot, or simply seeing how long someone could hang from a pull-up bar in the gym. It was like we were middle-school kids at recess, trying to outdo each other in everything. And as fun and crazy as it was, this competition within our team also made us better at pitting race cars. We were pushing one another. Challenging one another. And encouraging one another to be the very best each person could be.

Toward the end of the 2014 NASCAR season, we were approached by the team we are currently with while writing this book and were offered positions to be head pit crew coaches for the first time. This was a smaller team with a much leaner budget. Before we accepted the job, we sat down and wrote out everything we thought we would need to be successful. With our list complete, we went back to the race team and laid out what was absolutely essential and non-negotiable for us to agree to employment.

Our first non-negotiable was that we would have the freedom to create the environment we wanted to create. Now, that might not seem like a tall ask, but remember, we are talking about a sport rooted in Southern tradition with a history of a "my way or the highway" posture within racing organizations. Change does not come easy in NASCAR, so this non-negotiable wasn't a big deal—it was a *massive* deal. On the heels of our first demand, we also required their faith in us and the grace to allow the process to develop. Thus, our second non-negotiable was that they would have our backs as we tried to create that environment, regardless of whether or not they understood what was going on or what that might look like.

Before accepting the job, we took clear aim at bolstering the culture. We developed a schedule that was filled with team-building activities, volunteer events, hiking retreats in the mountains, and a handful of well-thought-out events that would create powerful moments within our environment. We had a wiffle-ball tournament on the opening day of Major League Baseball season. On July 1, Canada Day, we created a makeshift hockey rink crafted from all the racing tires in the shop and dedicated a day to playing hockey. Events like this were a huge departure from how this department was run in the past, and it was a risk. But it was a risk that was both calculated and necessary if we were to compete with the big teams. We wanted them to understand from the outset that if the owner pulled into the parking lot one day and saw our guys playing wiffle ball, we expected management to be willing to explain to him why the tournament needed to happen that day. Much to their credit, they agreed with it, and we signed our contracts.

One of the daily traditions we established (because our guys enjoyed it so much) was to play "Bump" or "Knockout" (as many call it) in the parking lot after we completed our drills and practice pit stops for the day. One day early in this process, the owner of our race team stepped outside while we were playing Bump. One of our veteran guys who had been a long-time employee within the company approached us in a panicked state, telling us that the boss was watching and that we should immediately get back to doing pit stops.

This was our moment. We either believed what we were doing was necessary enough to be willing to take on the boss if he disapproved or we didn't and reverted back to half-hearted pit stops to uphold an unproductive expectation. The game continued.

When the Big Bad Boss comes around—let's call him Jim—it usually strikes fear or anxiety within people. When we jokingly responded, "Who is Jim?" and kept playing, the message was clear. A good strategy is a good strategy regardless of who is paying attention. Fear is not a strategy and would not be welcomed in our environment. Culture is our strategy.

We see enjoyment and competition as cornerstones to a healthy culture. When you enjoy something you are going to both be better and get better at it. Everything in life runs more efficiently when it's fun, whether that's a marriage, a friendship, a workout group, or a book club. Enjoyment in the workplace eliminates drama, cultivates competition, and builds intimacy—a prerequisite of unity.

Integrity above All

Mornings at the racetrack come early. More often than not, the sun hasn't even revealed itself over the Turn 4 fence as crews busy themselves with pit-stall setup. Every race day, there is a laundry list of things that have to get accomplished. From setting up the pit box to prepping and gluing lug nuts onto the tires, there is an order to the work that necessitates everyone's best effort.

One cold February morning at Atlanta Motor Speedway, our crew was setting up the pit box, and we realized it was oddly quiet. One of our big culture guys, and arguably our loudest guy, was nowhere to be found. We asked the guys if they had seen him, and one of our guys told us that he had gone to the bathroom. Most racetracks have only one bathroom facility in the garage area for the 1,000-plus fans, pit crews, and mechanics on race day. So his absence was understandable.

Another ten or fifteen minutes went by, and he still had not returned. We figured something was up because he wasn't the kind of guy to skip out on work. As it turns out, he was cleaning the racetrack bathroom, which we found out from someone on another team who had seen him in there, scrubbing away. Apparently it wasn't up to the standards he had for himself or for fans who might be experiencing the racetrack for the first time. So he cleaned it.

As it's been said, integrity is what you do when no one else is watching. This guy isn't standard; he is exceptional. We believe in applying great patience and dedication when searching for the right pieces. As mentioned, we do this by carefully examining the ever-changing puzzle and identifying gaps in team chemistry, undergoing a thorough investigation of the individual, creating experiences that "remove the representative" and hiring based on one's ability to contribute to the whole.

How many times have talented people been derailed by a lack of integrity in the workplace? That boss who lies about the numbers and wrecks the company…or that coach who throws someone else under the bus to protect his or her own job…or that coworker who takes credit for something that someone else did.

Our goal is for our culture to be so grounded in integrity and effort that we are no longer needed as coaches. That's right—we will have done our job when we get replaced. These days, we are so confident in our guys and their character—and the culture they've created—that we know if we were called away from practice and couldn't make it out, our guys would take over and work just as hard without us there. Practice would go on as normal. That's how you know you have guys who are marked by integrity. When no one is looking, they keep moving forward, as individuals and as a team.

Soul vs. Ego

The only way to elevate the soul over the ego is through selflessness.

This is difficult to do in a hierarchical professional world that consists of people who are mostly motivated by advancement. What pulls the rope in most workplaces is the elevation and promotion of self (ego), not the elevation of others, purpose, heart, and mind (soul). It's no wonder that people feel so alone in most workplaces today. Interconnectedness gets lost when you have a team or company of people who are making decisions based on their ego's needs: what would be best for their own personal goals, not their coworkers' goals; what would be best for their personal image, not their team's.

Hierarchy is inevitable in company structures—or any group, for that matter, that needs organization to better manage its processes. But hierarchy becomes detrimental to an environment when it becomes a be-all, end-all motivating force—when people start to think that if they can just get that position, that raise, that award, that job, they'll have arrived. If you're living out of your ego, the easiest thing to do is to surround yourself with people who are exactly like you, further complicating the problem. Elevating the soul is how we re-establish belonging.

Human beings are at their best when they feel like they belong to something that is bigger than themselves. Connectedness speaks to our tribal biology. Show me somebody who feels like an outsider, like they are on an island in the workplace, and we'll show you someone who is stifled in their creativity and not expressing the fullness of their brilliance. How do you help people belong to something that is bigger than themselves in the workplace? Through people. Through relationships.

Returning to the story we told earlier about the executive who was brought in at a big company and immediately booted a woman out of her long-time office simply because he wanted an office with a window, we have talked about leading future team-building events through DECK and making the prize a single window from Lowe's. The purpose of this silly prize would simply be to ask these questions: "Why are you here? For yourself or for your teammates, for your ego or for this culture?" That's what a lot of people in the workplace do: they cut corners, they step on people, they use whatever power they have to assign maximum dominance to their title, just for an office with a window. Maybe our window would save them some time.

Modern C-suites have much to learn from the chiefs of old. The word "chief" has two meanings. One, as a noun, describes someone who is a leader of a people, group, or clan. The other is an adjective used to describe someone labeled as most important. Historically, the role of a chief is to protect, empower, and facilitate the flourishing of his or her tribe. Does that describe your boss? If you *are* the boss, does that describe you? It is no secret that a great many people in today's corporate climates are solely focused on rising to a C-level position. They will go to great lengths to self-promote, step over others, and even compromise their integrity to ascend to a desired position. We have always found this deeply disturbing, so we started challenging company executives with one simple question: "What does the *C* in *C-level* stand for?"

Most start by looking at us dumbfounded, wondering why we would ask a question with such a seemingly simple answer. "Everyone knows the *C* in *C-level* stands for chief," they reply.

We then ask, "How do you think a young Indian warrior ascended to the position of chief?" In their loss for words, we inform them that young Indian warriors were never concerned with becoming chief. Instead, their concern was on the overall health of the tribe. The young warriors were more worried about making sure they could provide food, shelter, and protection for the group. They worked tirelessly to ensure that the tribe thrived. And it was only through their selflessness and the respect that came from it that they ascended to the position of chief. They did not set out to become chief, but as the result of putting others before themselves, they became chief.

We then ask, "Do you know what the number one character trait of a psychopath is?"

The answer: profound lack of empathy.

So what more accurately describes the leadership today in most corporate climates? The Chief Executive Officer or the Psychopath Executive Officer? CEO or PEO? It is human nature to aspire to greatness. There is nothing wrong with wanting to one day rise to accept a C-Level position within a company. We are hired to help people develop their leadership style, and people often ask us what they need to do to get to the next level. The answer is simple: if you want to rise to a C-Level position, act like a chief.

From Selfishness to Awareness

At the conclusion of the 2017 NASCAR season, merely a day after the championship was awarded, it was announced that starting pit crews would be reduced from teams of six to teams of five. This was a shocking and unforeseen change that resulted in widespread cuts in pit crew positions across the sport. In an attempt to get ahead of the newly minted changes, we held practice the day after the announcement, two days before Thanksgiving.

Thanksgiving is typically a joyous week for us because it is the first holiday we have off since Easter. Our normally up-tempo, high-energy practice was decidedly somber, however, because everyone was acutely aware that at least four of their pit crew brothers would lose their jobs. Minutes after explaining our new reality to the group, an executive drove his Mclaren P1—a car worth well north of a million dollars—into our practice pit box and screeched to a halt right in front of us.

"Do you think you guys can pit this car?" he said jokingly.

Any other day, it might have been funny. But his disposition birthed a blindness that made him completely unaware of the fact that he was doing this to a department that had just found out that massive changes lay ahead. He was also one of the guys who approved this change.

Our group just stared at him. The respect he had from this group was lost in that moment.

If there's one thing that will rob an environment of nutrients, it's self-centeredness. One selfish person can destroy a culture, and several selfish people can destroy an entire company's environment, and, in turn, the company. A selfish act can feel like a direct punch in the face, forcing all affected to stammer backward, trying to regain their composure. A lot of people in leadership positions think they have to adopt a selfish, vehement, my-way-or-the-highway leadership style to get what they want, but they fail to see how inefficient and damaging it is in the long-term. Selfish acts evoke a deep-seated discontentment among those harmed. And what these acts ultimately demonstrate is a certain blindness and lack of empathy.

Self-centered acts, especially when they are committed by people in leadership positions, demonstrate to those affected that they do not have value. Nothing could be more destructive and toxic to the environment than failing to treat people as if they are valued. Because we as humans crave social connection and belonging—especially in spaces like the workplace in which we spend much of our time—selfishness cuts deep. Selfishness focuses on one plant in a garden, but you don't really have a garden if you have just one plant, or a few plants, with all the resources.

We've talked to many employees who often say they can be underpaid or overworked or undervalued, but not all three simultaneously. They can even be any two of the three, but definitely not all three. In a sport like ours, pay is often based on sponsorship dollars, there may be little wiggle room, and the hours are based squarely on the schedule dictated to us by NASCAR. How teams value employees, however, is an inside job. ROV (Return On Value) is an underrated metric of a company's long-term profitability. As a leader, the success of your environment depends on the value of care that you incorporate into your culture.

Think about the days, or years, when you were overworked and underpaid, yet you still enjoyed going to work. It wasn't a problem when it ignited your soul, when you were working for a cause you truly cared about.

We have had countless discussions with our "chiefs" over our years in racing in an attempt to help them put a finger on the pulse of the team. We have challenged them to care more. To incorporate simple measures into their daily routines like parking on varying sides of the building so they have to take different routes to their offices. This would allow them to encounter people in different departments on the way to their offices, and they could simply look people in their eyes to say, "Thank you for your work" along the way or drop off a few gift cards for coffee to a department that had to work overnight on a project. It takes selflessness and awareness to create these small, unexpected moments. It gets us back to the little things. After all, it is often the unexpected that we remember the most.

Advancing Based on Feedback

Business tycoon Elon Musk says one of the biggest factors to his success was and is his openness to criticism and feedback. "Constantly seek criticism," he says. "A well-thought-out critique of whatever you're doing is as valuable as gold."

So, with our egos in check, we go after every piece of negative feedback we can unearth. We schedule meetings where we discuss performance and position within the pit crews and give our guys an honest assessment of where they stand in the program. Even if the news is negative, we feel it helps build stronger pit crew members. Conversely, the conversation always ends with us allowing our guys to critique the program and our processes, as well as us as coaches. Though difficult to listen to sometimes, we used this negative feedback to lead us to some of the strongest parts of our current program.

Something we do every Thursday is open up the floor for our crews to talk. We ask them, "What questions, ideas, thoughts, complaints do you have for us from this week?" And then we wait…and wait. Often, someone speaks up. We want our guys to know that we deeply honor that space of constructive criticism. We also want to challenge them to be creative and think outside the box. We need their input for our culture to move forward.

Eventually someone might say, "Hey, I think we could be really good this weekend at the race if we can communicate more with one another leading up to the pit stops if we need to stop the car long or short, so we aren't on top of each other like last time we were at this race track" or "I didn't like how the schedule was communicated this week" or "I'm still disappointed with how our driver threw us under the bust last week because we never do that to him" or "We probably would have been better off with an extra practice session instead of the extra workout session this week" or "Can we not do drill day (Tuesday) like we did this week, since we didn't get much out of that?" Sometimes things are said that are tough to hear. A lot of times, it has to do with a mistake we made leadership-wise.

A scenario like this is scary for a lot of leaders to fathom because anything that comes up is often completely beyond their control and entails working through things as a team on the spot, rather than projecting orders downward. Some of the leaders we talk to respond to this idea with something like, "I could never do something like this because of the criticism I'd open myself up to." Well, you probably shouldn't be a leader, then.

What takes place during these weekly meetings is often unpredictable for us and involves conflict or difficult conversations. But this is where a lot of our growth as a team occurs. In the tension. How are you supposed to improve as a leader or as a team without the honest input of each person on your team?

Another thing we do to foster an open environment is incorporate honest evaluations at the end of each race season. We evaluate our guys, and then we have them evaluate both of us. And it's not just protocol. We take the evaluations seriously and talk at length with one another about how we can improve our leadership for the next race season.

Often, the hierarchical model of power is enforced over openness and collaboration. When people's opinions and input do not matter, how are they supposed to experience value, and how are others supposed to see what they're missing? Many of our teammates view their jobs as careers and callings, we think, because we actively listen to them and respond to their feedback through action. This "buy-in" is another key component of a healthy environment. We constantly want to know what they think and what they're seeing that we might not see.

Feedback is crucial to helping an environment remain healthy. Even negative feedback, which at times can be uncomfortable to hear, has the potential to move a culture forward. Negative feedback is a luxury that should be cherished because no one person or process is perfect. Feedback shows where there is room for growth and improvement. Truly listening requires openness, humility, and a hunger to steadily evolve and improve as a team. Ignoring negative feedback or discounting its value is a fool's game. So often in toxic cultures, leaders would rather be ruined by praise than saved by criticism. Increase your capacity for feedback, and the perceived threats from the criticism will be muted by the roar of the opportunities.

Experts vs. Listeners

Irish philosopher and author Peter Rollins says he enjoys organizing "evangelism teams" in Northern Ireland—not to evangelize to people, but rather to be evangelized. Rollins's group of mostly Christians visits different faith communities, and they honestly ask those communities how Christians are perceived, what their blind spots are, and what they need to learn. They simply *listen and learn.* They aren't out to prove anything. They aren't out to convert anyone. They have no agenda. Their only goal is to grow—through listening and learning. This is a countercultural disposition in a world filled with people who often just want to share or voice their opinions.

We are not expert pit crew coaches. We don't have it all figured it out. We have plenty of blind spots. Each week, we make our fair share of mistakes. But we own every misstep. The most toxic thing for a person in a leadership position to believe is that he or she is an expert with the best solution for every question. Yet this is what many are tempted to believe because of their position. When the ego is running the show, the temptation for a leader is to believe that he or she needs to hold everything together rather than listen to those who are holding the company together, to have it all figured out rather than learn from those who have different perspectives within the company. Ego convinces you that it's all up to you, when in all reality, it should be up to you to listen and learn from those you are leading. The best leaders are the best listeners.

Approachability

When we became pit crew coaches, one of the few things we were dogmatic about on race day was refraining from celebrating. Watch any NASCAR race, and you'll see pit crews celebrating after a fast stop on pit row. There were a number of pit crews that showboated and made absolute fools of themselves after a good pit stop, and we wanted to be different. We were entirely against it. We were probably mostly afraid that if our guys started celebrating a fast pit stop, they would look like imbeciles if they were to have a slower pit stop later. We are both big believers that you shouldn't let outcomes get you too high or too low. There is karmic balance in sports between humility and elation.

A couple of times, our guys celebrated after a good pit stop, and we found ourselves rebuking them in some way, cautioning them to not let their emotions get out of control. At a fall Martinsville race, one of our superstars was celebrating pretty excessively, and neither of us was happy about it. We didn't say anything, but one of our first-year guys noticed our apparent disappointment. Later that day, after the race, he politely asked us why we were so against it. We told him our reason—that celebrating felt like showboating and seemed arrogant, to which he replied, "What if celebrating after a good pit stop is the culmination of all the hard work we put in? Don't you think we should have the right to be able to express that joy because of the hours we put into this, as long as it's not disrespectful?"

Celebrating had always been a non-negotiable to us, but neither of us could answer his thoughtful questions. We asked if we could take some more time to think about it and give him an answer the next day. We discussed his thoughts thoroughly with one another, knowing we had to give him an answer.

What we ultimately decided was that we were projecting too much of our own personalities and life experiences onto those we were coaching. Neither of us had celebrated in our respected sports whenever we scored or had a big play, nor had we celebrated on the various pit crews we had worked with. But we realized that we were acting as if we had the universally correct approach, just because of our own belief system. We told him that his idea had merit, and then we told the team about our change of heart.

To this day, both of us still sometimes find ourselves cringing when we see our guys celebrating. Neither of us, frankly, understands it. But we also don't want to rob them of that moment of elation, a moment they worked so hard for, a moment they deserve to celebrate. And it ultimately makes us better as a team because they are able to more freely express themselves. Any time you can make space for someone's true self to shine, the more you are going to get that person's best self.

We have also been on the other side of this problem, too. All the big shops that NASCAR teams call home are a distant cry from your local mechanic's shop. These teams are housed in beautiful glass buildings, with polished white floors—not a spot of grease to be found anywhere! Sitting above the shop floor are myriad gorgeous meeting spaces and offices that house the executive team that oversees race operations. Like most large companies, every office takes on a note of similarity, being neatly provisioned with a desk and a chair. It's likely adorned with personal effects like family pictures, children's drawings, artwork, and maybe even a plant or two. What is also similar is that every desk within an office faces the door so that the office's inhabitant can welcome anyone who enters his or her office.

Well, this was not the case at one of our race teams. The highest-ranking executive in our building, our president, sat with his back to his office door. When you walked into his office, you immediately felt like you were burdening him or interrupting him by your sheer presence. We politely mentioned to him that he might want to consider moving his desk so that it was facing the door, thus creating a more open, inviting mood, but it never happened. Not heeding our advice demonstrated his inability to advance based on feedback. But more than that, his overall posture, evidenced by his back to the door, showed that he wasn't approachable. He already had all the answers.

We share both of these stories back-to-back, not to shame that executive but rather to relate to him. When it came to our guys celebrating, our egos hated the possibility that we might be wrong and what was most comfortable for us (not celebrating) might not be the best rule for the men we were leading. It's difficult when you're in a leadership position and you realize you've been doing something all wrong. It's humbling. But that's part of being a leader. Poor leaders never let themselves experience this kind of vulnerability. Admitting that you are wrong or that you don't know the answer to a question adds a humanness to leaders that makes them more relatable to those they lead.

These days, we are happy to admit when we are wrong. We want someone to approach us and point out a blind spot we have. Why? Because that means that we get to grow and make things better for our environment. Though we've failed many times as coaches, we're learning to listen more so we can learn more. Approachability makes room for positive and worthwhile change.

The Buffer

As a leader, you are tasked with making difficult decisions…and once you make a decision, you are rewarded with the opportunity to make another difficult decision. As a leader, you will be faced with endless difficult decisions. If your shoulders aren't broad enough or your skin isn't thick enough for that, you may want to consider something other than leadership. The truth is that if you were to really examine why people want to climb the corporate ladder or advance in their careers, you'd probably find that they aren't ready to be true leaders. Maybe they want a specific position to get a raise or to drive a company car—ego things—but they are unprepared for the responsibility that comes with making difficult decisions.

The default reaction in the racing world, often, isn't to make the difficult decisions; it's to project in order to protect—to *project* downward in the hierarchical structure to *protect* your own position and your own ego. Most people's fears and detractors rise up out of their own egos. We have a rule in our pit crew department that we have long held on to that we refuse to hold counsel with our fears or our detractors. We've committed to never projecting things downward whenever upper management yells at us. Even if it was one of our guys who made the mistake, we've decided to take responsibility for our own decision making as coaches, as long as our guys are adopting the right mindset, giving their best effort each day, and working with integrity at the forefront.

The year after NASCAR made sweeping changes to the way pit stops were executed, we were struggling as a racing team, and the pit crew got off to a slow start. Those above us told us that we needed to make sure our guys kept working throughout our week off. It's really easy to use the pit crew as a scapegoat because their part is very visible and held against a time metric that ticks away on a television screen as they perform their task. We simply told management "no." We disagreed that more work was the answer, believing that some time away would renew our focus and benefit us further down the road. Our guys had worked through their off-season, normally a time for rest, and needed a break. We were determined not to keep projecting downward just for the sake of appeasing those above us. We knew that the anger toward us would only be amplified if we didn't perform well the rest of the season.

All these leadership principles are difficult in creating a healthy environment because it can feel incredibly personal. We're just as guilty as the next person at taking things personally. Being a protective layer and buffer between management and those who you are leading results in even more criticism and attacks. Our jobs as coaches are important to us; it's frustrating sometimes to take the beating. But that goes back to self-care. When it feels personal, you meditate. You ask yourself the hard questions. You enter into introspection. You ask yourself, "Is my frustration in any way related to my ego?"

Everyone likes shade on a brutally hot summer day. The shade provides comfort in the intensity of the heat. As a leader, you might need to take the blame and criticism—the heat—so that others feel safe where they are and give their best out of a place of security rather than fear. We are determined to keep creating space for our group to showcase their best attitudes and efforts. If we want them to unleash their best selves, then we have to make that space, as leaders, for them to do so. We want to provide shade.

8

Vertical Thinking

The front changer grabs spokes on the wheel. With the jack securely under the car, the jackman prepares to press the handle to the ground, lifting the car. The carrier moves toward a new left-front tire being rolled toward the car. The rear changer strikes lug nut four of five. The gasman steps over the tire changer's air hose while plugging in the second can of fuel.

-The 8th second of a NASCAR pit stop

We knew from the onset of taking over a dysfunctional pit crew program that we had to think vertically. Time and processes unfold linearly, but vertical thinking is about taking a single point in time, or within a process, and exploring its unfathomable heights and depths. It's about thinking outside the box as it pertains to processes and transcending tradition. It's about unleashing the depth of your own heart and mind for purpose, not just using your hands and feet for labor.

Vertical thinking is about seeing the potential in everything. It's a new set of glasses in the workplace, a new lens for reality. It's about adopting a north-and-south posture (unleashing the fullness of your mind, heart, and energy), not just the standard east-and-west posture (focusing on where you're going, what there is to do, or where you have gone). *Horizontal* thinking is the how. *Vertical* thinking is the why.

Most workplaces consist of people who have the mindset that they are operating on an assembly line. It's all about production, the destination, and profitability. Each person on that horizontal assembly line has a specific task in the process. Each task has to be done for deadlines to be hit and production goals to be met. All of this is normal, natural, and needed for a company to stay afloat. But incorporating vertical thinking into our natural horizontal reality requires a different mindset.

A horizontal thinker says, "I'm going to clock as many hours as I can so my boss will notice me," but a vertical thinker asks, "How can I raise the bar for this company? What are we not seeing that could elevate us to the next level?" A vertical thinker dives into that point and makes the most of it.

A lot of people who are perfectionistic—beating themselves up for their past mistakes—or destination-oriented—obsessing over the future—miss out on the many points of opportunity each day. A vertical thinker asks these types of questions: "What self-care techniques can I implement in my life so I can be present with the task at hand and healthier in the workplace?" or "How can I make this process more efficient and beneficial to everyone?" or "How can I be there for the person next to me, who seems to be having a bad day or seems to not be able to keep pace with the rest of the team?"

Vertical thinking happens in healthy environments and cultures, where people are inspired to break out of the cycle of common thought and rise above the status quo. Creativity and innovation are born in environments that cultivate vertical thinking. Deep relationships and meaningful communication are fostered in vertical-thinking environments because excellence is elevated over perfectionism. Vertical thinkers rise above the daily malaise and make their tasks, moments, and interactions purposeful. It's a mindset and a posture that changes you and your company.

The Most Dangerous Phrase in the English Language

It took three races into our coaching careers to challenge the status quo within the racing culture.

At Las Vegas Motor Speedway, the garage usually opens early...really early: six o'clock in the morning early. The mechanics who oversee the operation and setup of these cars need every bit of that time to get the car prepared for the race. For years, pit crews have just followed suit and arrived at the same time, rushing to set up their pit boxes and equipment, only to then sit around for the next four hours. We told our guys that they could get some extra rest and be at the track at eight o'clock instead of six. The six o'clock racetrack tradition served our athletes no purpose whatsoever.

As our team walked onto the track together, every single pit box was set up except for our pit boxes. Walking in was unnerving at first, as we, a collection of misfits and the overlooked, led by two rookie pit crew coaches, walked past the garage. We could feel people's eyes on us. It was as if they were saying, "A little late, aren't you?" or "Get here when you can!"

There was a brief moment when we questioned whether or not we had made the correct decision. Were we doing the right thing? Did we take things too far? Was tampering with race-day traditions and routines too radical of a move for rookie coaches? Who did we think we were?

But we kept saying to ourselves, *No, we're doing the right thing.*

Why wouldn't we want our guys to be more rested? Why would we want them standing around for three or four hours? It is our belief that our bosses are not paying us to mindlessly follow what everybody else is doing—*they are paying us to think*. We wanted to do anything we could to give our guys a mental and emotional edge. Positioning them to have more energy was a good place to start.

Horizontal thinking is doing the same thing and not knowing why you're doing it. Vertical thinking is about challenging the status quo and tradition—not for rebellion's sake, but to improve how things are done. Think about all the apps for our digital devices that have been developed in recent years because someone in the tech world was willing to challenge how things have always been done. Instead of finding or calling a taxi, order an Uber or a Lyft with two clicks on your phone. Instead of paying an outrageous price on a hotel, stay in someone's house or apartment through Airbnb. Instead of waiting for the bus or the train that will take you to a specific stop, find a Bird or Lime scooter that you can ride wherever you want.

One of the quotes we often share is, "The path is made in the walking of it." You can't just walk through the woods once and call it a trail, especially if you want others to follow that trail for themselves. You have to keep walking it and consider that what brought you success yesterday might not bring you success today. The trail evolves the more you walk it. It takes intention, time, and energy.

We believe the most dangerous phrase in the English language is, "This is the way we have always done it." Too many people in the workplace have been walking the same unfulfilling or uninspiring trail that has been there for years, either too terrified or too comfortable to step off and blaze a new trail. This is how companies get stuck and eventually fold—because of their inability to change and evolve…because of their unwillingness to let those in their company shape a new path to the beautiful place that is calling to them.

Someone is waiting for you to find a new route and blaze a new trail. Their fulfillment and livelihood is dependent on it. For the vertical thinker, the danger of reward overpowers the danger of risk. So get off the trail of comfort when opportunities present themselves and get dangerous. Get vertical.

Titles Are for Books

When we became coaches, we wanted to make sure that one of the cornerstones in our culture was volunteering. Volunteering impacts your community, expands your perspective, deepens your purpose and sense of fulfillment, and connects you with those around you.

Around the holidays our first year, one of the things we wanted to implement was a charitable initiative called "The Race to the North Pole." Basically, it was a workout competition where teams were assembled using reindeer names. It was the objective of those on Team Rudolph to accumulate miles that got them to the North Pole (or farther): one mile for every minute they worked out, five miles for every canned food item they donated, double the workout miles when they donated a toy, and triple the workout miles when they donated a bike. Most importantly, the goal was to overwhelm Ronald McDonald House with toys and bikes that they could give to the families they served around Christmas.

Strangely, however, the first year we wanted to implement this, higher-ups within the company told us that we weren't allowed to do so.

We wanted to set up a Christmas tree in the lobby and make it a company-wide initiative, but they told us no. We were actually discouraged from doing it at all. Why? We got the feeling that they didn't want this outreach to be a distraction to the team and that they didn't see how it could possibly benefit our efficiency and productivity.

Well, as less-than-ideal listeners in moments like those, we decided to go ahead with the Race to the North Pole anyway among the pit crew department, despite knowing that we might be reprimanded for blatantly disobeying. Our department, and a handful of other mechanics and marketing folks, really bought into it and latched onto the vision. At the conclusion of the contest, we showed up at the local Ronald McDonald House with boxes upon boxes of canned food, two carloads of toys, and three truckloads full of children's bicycles.

Where this gets interesting is that McDonald's just happened to be a sponsor on one of our race team's cars. That was not our intention, but it did shine a favorable light on our race team. The administration team at the Ronald McDonald House was so overwhelmed with the magnitude of the delivery that they splashed pictures all over social media, thanking our race team for its kindness. And guess who the first ones were to share or retweet Ronald McDonald House's social media posts? Correct—the same executives who told us we couldn't implement the Race to the North Pole within the company. Now they were the ones who were lauding praise on us on social media because it made their racing team look good.

This story highlights how we have gotten it wrong, at times, in the workplace. We forget what it means to be truly successful when we are buried in tasks. We were originally told that we couldn't spearhead the initiative, most likely because leadership believed it would hurt our productivity—*horizontal thinking*. Vertical thinking weaves purpose into productivity, and empathy into efficiency.

Some people want to make an impact in their workplace but think they have to have a certain title or position before they can effect change. Part of vertical thinking, however, is making an impact right where you are, at the point where you are at *right now*. Titles are for books, not human beings. We wanted to make the Race to the North Pole a company-wide initiative but were told we couldn't. So we did it within our pit crew department and blew Ronald McDonald House away. And now it's something the entire company does every holiday season. You can affect your culture right where you're at. Don't let the lack of a title deter you from doing great things.

Vertical thinking is not vertical advancement. It can be a by-product but shouldn't be the focus. The animating force behind most people's workplace efforts is to climb in some way, whether that's the corporate ladder or to a new office or to a new level of respect or responsibility within a company. Whenever someone realizes he or she is gifted, the most natural question to ask is, "How can I monetize this or use this to shape my own perception or reputation within my company?" The most inspirational people we know are the ones who want to dive in, help, and impact people right where they are. Vertical thinkers help *others* climb.

Investing in Yourself

After our first season as coaches, both of our bodies physically crashed from exhaustion. We didn't realize how little time we had taken for ourselves until after the season was already over. Forty straight weeks of twelve-hour days, trying to turn a dumpster fire into a competitive pit crew department, had taken its toll. The season had been filled with putting out fires, trying to establish a new culture, and making a number of necessary personnel changes. As is the case for a lot of people who start their own company or begin a new position, our first year felt like we were constantly reacting to things. Each day was filled with new challenges, meetings, emails, phone calls, recruiting dinners, film sessions, tough conversations, more meetings, etc.

We realized very quickly in the off-season that if we wanted to continue to establish a healthy culture rooted in integrity, effort, and enjoyment, then we first needed to take care of ourselves. How could we invest in others if we had no energy to give? How could we think outside the box if we were just trying to keep our heads above water?

It's difficult to think vertically if you're not taking care of yourself.

Burnout is more common than ever before in America today. A 2016 General Society Survey, which tracked behaviors and attitudes in the American workplace since 1972, cited that 50 percent of respondents are consistently exhausted because of work. Two decades before, that number was only 18 percent.[7] Overwork is prevalent in America.

According to Brad Stulberg, coauthor of *Peak Performance: Elevate Your Game, Avoid Burnout, and Thrive with the New Science of Success*, Americans work more hours in the evenings and on the weekends than most other populations. The emergence of smartphones also generally made Americans on call because of how often they check their phones and how their bosses can contact them any hour of the day or night.

But it's not just an American problem. The Japanese, known for their productivity and efficiency, are so work-obsessed that it is leading to relational neglect. They are the first modern society that is on pace to be extinct. The estimated number of babies born in Japan in 2018 dropped to the lowest number since comparable data became available in 1899, government figures from Japan showed in December 2018. The figure for the year was estimated at 921,000, down 25,000 from 2017, staying below the one million mark for the third straight year, according to the Ministry of Health, Labor and Welfare. Deaths during the year totaled an estimated 1.37 million, a postwar record high, with a natural population decline of 448,000, the largest ever. The data show the pace of population decline is picking up amid the falling birthrate, suggesting it is increasingly difficult for the government to attain its goal of raising the total fertility rate to 1.8 by the end of fiscal 2025.[8]

One reason why Japan's population is declining is that it is becoming increasingly common for Japanese couples to remain in sexless marriages. In 2016, a survey by the Japan Family Planning Association found that 53.4 percent of male and 48.8 percent of female respondents said they had had no sexual intercourse during the previous month. When asked to cite their reasons for being uninterested in sex, the most common reason among married men, at 35.2 percent, was that they were "too tired from work." Among women, the most common reason cited, at 22.3 percent, was that sex is "too much hassle."[9]

[7.] "Burnout at Work Isn't Just about Exhaustion. It's Also About Loneliness," Emma Seppälä and Marissa King, *Harvard Business Review*, June 29, 2017, https://hbr.org/2017/06/burnout-at-work-isnt-just-about-exhaustion-its-also-about-loneliness.

[8.] "Number of Babies Born in Japan in 2018 Lowest Since Records Began; Population Decline the Highest," Kyodo, *The Japan Times*, December 18, 2019, https://www.japantimes.co.jp/news/2018/12/21/national/number-babies-born-japan-2018-lowest-since-records-began-population-decline-highest/#.XB0GwktKiUm.

[9.] "Survey Finds Record Number of 'Sexless' Married Couples in Japan," nippon, February 23, 2017, https://www.nippon.com/en/features/h00161/survey-finds-record-number-of-sexless-married-couples-in-japan.html.

The stress from burnout drives us away from others, not toward them.

Meaning is found in relationships, but the workplace is trending toward becoming non-relational. *Little synergy.* The workplace is a space where teams have the opportunity to accomplish something together, but more than half of the people in the American workplace, studies show, are burnt out and exhausted. *Little energy.* Good leaders need a daily self-care routine so that they can have the energy to invest in those they are leading and in their relationships with them. We both go through routines every morning to make sure we are charged up and ready for each day.

We know we can't lead each of our individuals or groups in the exact same way. They all have different personalities and learning styles. Some of them are like gigantic cruise ships—with big personalities and big ideas, but it takes them a long time to get going. Others are like Jet Skis—eager, quick-thinking, and strong out of the gate. Both the cruise ships and Jet Skis eventually run out of fuel. This is why we have a few sailboats—those who are more calculated, slower, perhaps boring, but often the only ones who are in motion. Each person requires different kinds of fuel or strategy to partner with his or her movement. We know we can't just show up. It's not enough. And if we aren't invested in ourselves—charged up, fueled up, and ready to go—it will be more difficult to pour out overflow into others. The best way to pour into others is to fully pour into yourself and let it overflow into the lives around you. If you're not invested in yourself, it can't trickle down to anyone else. Vertical thinking hinges on self-care.

The Greatest Plan Ever

Imagine someone who is on deck to become the next boss, coach, manager, or director. This person is bursting with enthusiasm, excited to execute his or her "Greatest Plan Ever"—something the person has worked hard to develop while eagerly awaiting a position of leadership. The person eventually gets the desired position and shows up on the first day, determined to implement the Greatest Plan Ever. But before this person can implement the plan, his or her morning is consumed by multiple well-wishers, the IT department setting up a new computer, and the CEO stopping by to offer her congratulations. Lunch flies by, there are three fires to put out in the afternoon, and before you know it, everyone has left for the day. "The Greatest Plan Ever" gets delayed a day.

The next day, the person has to proverbially photocopy the Greatest Plan Ever to bring it back—it's the same plan but is a little lighter because it's photocopied. Day 2, however, looks a lot like Day 1: chaos. Personnel changes. Lunch with this person. A meeting with that person. And, before the person knows it, once again, the day is over, and his or her plan still has not been introduced. The pace of business necessitates this pace, but the Greatest Plan Ever is photocopied and fades with every passing day.

A whole year goes by, and by now the Greatest Plan Ever that has been photocopied over and over, showing up lighter each day, is now just a blank piece of paper.

The general manager at our first race shop epitomized this example. He would enter each day with all these plans and grand ideas, but when it came time for us to actually implement his ideas, he was impossible to get in touch with to authorize anything—he'd have multiple meetings every day, along with all kinds of corporate tasks. His Greatest Plan Ever would get buried in structure and duty. He didn't make the space for himself to avoid being reactive throughout each workday. The excessive musical-chairs dance from meeting to meeting stressed him into a state of survival. There was a multiyear span in which process closed more windows of opportunity than any person or lack of a resource. He mistook activity for achievement.

Each of us enters the day with a plan of execution in some way, but if you don't make time for yourself to think vertically, the plan will never get implemented. Or you implement the plan and experience success but then run the same play every day, every year, without evolving or adapting. In both cases, you eventually end up with a blank piece of paper.

People Aren't Machines

When I (Metcalf) was a freshman football player, one of my teammates, an offensive lineman, dislocated his ankle during practice so badly that his foot spun around 180 degrees. He was lying on his stomach, writhing in pain, but his toes were pointing straight up toward the sky. Practice came to a stop. All of our teammates were in shock. Seconds later, we all heard a booming, commanding voice: "Move the drill up twenty yards, on the ball!"

It was the offensive coordinator, yelling from a golf cart on the sidelines over a megaphone, demanding that we run the next play ASAP. We looked at the coach, shocked, as if to say, "Do you *not* see what's happening right now?"

"Get the trainer for number fifty-five!" the coach yelled, not even calling the player by name, "and move it up twenty yards. *On. The. Ball!*"

Here were all these kids who were busting their butts for their coach on a hot summer day in August, and in that brief interaction, the coach showed all of us his cards. He didn't care about us as people. He only wanted to use us and our abilities for his football program.

This is horizontal thinking: caring only about his team's performance in practice that day and how it might affect his goals for the program and the linear direction he wanted to take the team that year. Vertical thinking sees the depth of each person. Their struggles. Their joys. Their unique personalities. Most certainly, their names. This could have been an easy opportunity for connection but instead became a source of division.

One of the tire changers whose performance helped build our program seemed to sometimes struggle during different physical activities. On our annual hike to Mt. LeConte, we noticed that he was often lagging behind the group, struggling to keep up. He was a hard worker, so we feared that something might be going on in his body.

So, during our team's annual physicals that year, we had EKGs ordered for each person within the pit crew department. The racing team didn't want to pay for it, but we ordered it anyway…and we sent them the invoice. We had the most physically demanding jobs in the company, and each person should know whether or not his heart was healthy. It just seemed like common sense.

Turns out, the guy who had been struggling while hiking in the mountains (who also had a wife and son, by the way) had a major heart condition with a couple of failing heart valves. He needed to go in for immediate surgery. Though the racing team didn't want to fund the EKGs, it would have been much more expensive had something terrible happened to him, not to mention a public relations nightmare. And, most importantly, this was a human life we were talking about, not a machine who was there to simply work for a racing team.

People in leadership positions who just use those who they are leading as ends to a means in their plan to make themselves or their company shine are thinking plainly, within two limited planes. Vertical thinkers, however, help position individuals to shine *outside* those planes.

Leaving the Ninety-Nine

One of our first hires was a tire changer who had actually been with the company before we were hired but had not made a good impression. Many within the company saw him as a troublemaker, and many people above us questioned the decision to bring him back. We had thoroughly vetted him, and we knew he was a high-character guy who had a lot of energy and talent—why wouldn't we consider hiring him? Maybe he just needed a new environment to really shine.

After his first month, it turns out that new air and soil were exactly what he needed. We communicated our expectations with him and told him what he was up against at the start. He worked hard to rebuild his reputation and unleash his best self. Many people eventually ended up saying to us, "You were right about him; he's like a completely different person."

One day, however, we were supposed to host a company-wide meeting about culture—a real chance to show everyone in the company what we were about—but right before the meeting, someone accused the guy of something he didn't do. He was extremely hurt by the accusation. He was being accused of something that his old self might have done…but not his best self that was really thriving in the environment he was in. He became confrontational and combative when he was accused of being the person he once was. He needed to be heard. He needed the attention of one of us.

Though it was important that both of us were at the company-wide culture meeting, we decided it was more important for one of us to be with this guy who had worked hard to rebuild his reputation and was in a lot of pain. The culture meeting ended up being a debacle, as we had only practiced our talk together. The decision for both of us not to be at the meeting definitely had a recklessness and foolishness to it because it was our chance to introduce some new mindsets and postures to the entire racing team. But the truth is that gravitating toward the one, and leaving the ninety-nine, *is* our culture.

That company-wide meeting is still something that people joke with us about because of how disastrous it was. It is probably why management thinks we should "focus on pit stops." We were good then and are better now because we have learned from such failures. That taught us to know each other's content before going into meetings or presentations: vertical thinking.

We wish we could forget some of these embarrassing moments, but that tire changer will never forget—no matter where he goes in his career or in life—that there are people who believe in him and will always be in his corner.

Transparency

NASCAR tire changers are an odd bunch. Much like a goal-tender in hockey or a kicker in football, they have a highly technical and difficult skill they must perform with a moment's notice. And anything less than perfection is considered a failure. They are tasked with hitting five lug nuts in under a second. This takes immense focus to execute. This often leads to these guys being mischaracterized as quirky, shy, or just plain odd.

One day, we noticed that a starting tire changer was a little bit behind during practice. He was on pattern, but he was just a hair slow when he was changing lug nuts. We sat down with him to see what was going on. Eventually, we got him to reluctantly admit to us that the carrier's shoulder was slightly in the way and that he was struggling to see a specific lug nut. He didn't want to say anything because, one, he didn't like confrontation, and, two, he didn't want to throw his teammate, whom he liked, under the bus. We brought everyone over and had the changer ask the carrier, in front of everyone, what he needed him to do. "I can't promise, but I'll try," the carrier said.

Almost immediately, that subtle change led to us picking up another two-tenths of a second. It might seem minuscule, but as we discussed earlier, that extra two-tenths of a second of speed could be the difference in a million dollars at the Daytona 500. Sometimes that two-tenths-of-a-second transparency is the extra 1 percent that can push your company to the next level. Matt Chandler, pastor and author, once said, "To be 99 percent known is to be unknown."

The workplace is generally obsessed with image and with keeping conflict and tension at its lowest—that's why full transparency is often feared or avoided. But a culture that leads people to suppress what they think or feel ultimately leads to a tension that is constantly building beneath the surface. Eventually there will be an explosion. A lot of people in leadership positions mislead themselves and think that things will be better by avoiding the tension. But if you want to lead a high-performing team, the issues aren't going to just go away because you didn't talk about them.

One of the biggest misconceptions of high-performing teams is that they are devoid of conflict. This could not be further from the truth. All teams are rife with conflict, but what separates high-performing teams from other teams is their ability to manage this conflict. It's up to leaders to create a healthy environment where those who they are leading have the space and freedom to talk about anything they think is important to the chemistry or high-functioning aspect of the team. Leaders need to be hyper-aware of the different personalities, tendencies, and possible tensions at play.

A horizontal thinker fears that managing tension or conflict will take up too much time, negatively impact productivity, or hurt the image of the company. A vertical thinker is transparent and willing to have those conversations because it makes everyone better and elevates the company as a whole. Transparency multiplies itself. When one person is transparent, it lets someone else know that he or she can also be transparent. This open communication moves the entire team forward. Our tire changer felt better individually because he finally stopped suppressing his frustration and verbalized it; our tire carrier felt better individually because he learned how he could improve and also knew that he had the freedom to express his own frustration in the future. Our team was ultimately better for it.

Acknowledging Sacrifice

A couple years ago, our team was putting together a championship season. All the mechanics on the shop floor were dedicating long hours of preparation, when a battery caught fire on the shop floor. A fire in a race shop is everyone's worst nightmare but is surprisingly not all that uncommon. It's terrifying because of the surrounding fuel tanks and other combustibles on hand in most garages.

Three mechanics who were underneath the car were quick to act. They yanked the battery from the car, threw it onto a cart, and rushed it out of the building and into the parking lot. The very moment they got the battery outside, one of the mechanics collapsed onto the grass and began throwing up. He had inhaled so much smoke that he immediately began puking his guts out into the grass.

With the crisis averted, and two of the three mechanics on their hands and knees simply trying to breathe, just feet from the front door, the team president walked outside. It was late in the day, and he was apparently in a rush. We saw the president walk right past the mechanic who was puking, hit the key fob for his eighty-thousand-dollar car, hop in, and leave…without saying a word. These guys had just prevented a major catastrophe from happening at the president's multimillion-dollar facility where he ran his multimillion-dollar operation, and he was too uninterested to even acknowledge their sacrifice.

The fire was a big deal, but the president's absolute indifference to the guys in distress on the grass was the topic of just about every afternoon conversation. What people had always suspected about the president was suddenly confirmed: he was all about himself…and he didn't care about his employees, other than paying them to do a job. How out of touch do you have to be with reality—with your own humanity—to act that way? Yet it's a perfect example of what can become commonplace in the American workplace without transparency: coldness, lack of empathy, and the prevalence of relational apathy.

Perhaps in the president's performance-driven, goal-consumed mind, these heroic men didn't do anything to exceed his expectations because he never foresaw his building burning down to begin with. Maybe in the president's mind, these brave men were just "doing their job," the job he paid them to do. He didn't see their efforts affecting his bottom line (even though their efforts saved his bottom line). It wouldn't surprise us if he was upset because one of his car batteries was ruined. And so their sacrifice went unacknowledged by the most important person in the company because he didn't even see it as sacrifice. Maybe the president was on the way to an important meeting that would directly benefit those mechanics and had their best interests in mind. Yet, how difficult would it have been to simply say, "Thank you"? Most in the workplace are not necessarily seeking a raise for their great efforts; they are just seeking to know that they matter, that someone above them cares.

We try to recognize that the life that our guys live during the season is a hard one. The grueling NASCAR schedule runs from Valentine's Day until Thanksgiving. From February to November, there are only two weekends off. Our group is away from their families on most holidays and weekends.

But we want our team to know that amid the chaos of the season, they are deeply valued and not taken for granted. We want them to know that we see their sacrifice and dedication because we have lived them ourselves. It's easy for a lot of people in our industry to dismiss pit crew members' challenges. It's not uncommon to hear people utter things like, "This is the life they chose" or "They get two months off during the winter." Frankly, it *is* the life they chose, and they *do* get two months off during the winter, but that doesn't mean that the lifestyle doesn't come without challenges and frustrations. When we are more demanding of them in a space that is already demanding, it rarely inspires anything exceptional. But when we care about them as people and relate to their challenges, it builds mutual understanding between employees and the employer.

We've all probably heard someone utter the phrase "That's their job" or "They get paid to do that." That was exactly the answer from a driver we pitted for after winning a notable race in 2014. We put him in position to win that race. One day, when he placed the order for the championship rings for a few of his close friends, a senior team member asked him if he was going to buy rings for the pit crew guys. We will never forget the driver saying, "They got paid to be there. They did their jobs. I'm not getting them anything."

Every person on this earth has a limited amount of time and energy in their day, and if they've chosen to use their time and energy in a way that makes your life in the workplace easier and more comfortable, doing something that you can't do yourself, that effort deserves to be acknowledged and applauded. When we have the mindset that everyone is here to simply do their job, we muffle out the sounds of gratitude that resound in high-performing teams. Attitudes of gratitude will invoke appreciation within and inspire it in others. It's impossible to ignore something you are truly grateful for.

An Avenue for Service and Kindness

To say the least, we felt out of place. We sat there at a lavish, suit-and-tie NASCAR event in a ballroom at the Loews Hotel in South Beach, Florida. An elegant purple hue dimly lit the room, as servers walked by handing out cocktails and hors d'oeuvres.

We were sitting at a table with three of the guys on our pit crew and two of the higher-ups at our race team. Our pit crew had been nominated for the 2017 Comcast Community Award, an annual award given to someone (or a group) in NASCAR who had notably given back to their local community. It's NASCAR's version of the NFL's Walter Payton Award. Though our guys had certainly done a lot of volunteering and charity work throughout the year, whether it was at Meals on Wheels, a nearby orphanage, a local elementary school, or the Ronald McDonald House, we were surprised that a pit crew had been nominated. We didn't even know that a pit crew *could* be nominated.

Nearby were tables with the other two nominees, who happened to be two of the most talented and popular drivers in racing: seven-time Cup Series champion Jimmie Johnson and two-time Cup Series champion Brad Keselowski. Did a pit crew really have a chance at winning a community award if it was going up against the stardom of Johnson and Keselowski?

It had been a tumultuous few weeks, performance-wise, leading up to the ceremony. First was the Charlotte race in mid-October, where we had helped our top driver jump to first-place with a fast pit stop, only to fall to twelfth at the next stop, when one of our tire carriers tripped over the air hose. We finished tenth that fall evening. We were having an outstanding year, our top driver having won a career-high four times, and we were entering the playoffs contending for a championship, on the doorstep of winning the prestigious Monster Energy NASCAR Cup. Our unfortunate luck reappeared two weeks after Charlotte, in Kansas, where an unlikely motor failure seventy-three laps into the race resulted in our driver unexpectedly falling out of championship contention. Following that were two crashes in consecutive races at Martinsville and Texas. And last, a nonwork-related event occurred that did not correspond to the values we held ourselves and our guys to. We were seconds away from resigning until we were promised that something would be done immediately once we were back at headquarters. Our performance was struggling, and because of that, our culture was now being micromanaged by higher-ups.

In just a few weeks, we had gone from being one of the favorites to win the Monster Energy NASCAR Cup to legitimately wanting to quit our jobs. It was a disappointing end to an outstanding year for our race team and a difficult way for our pit crew department to end the season. We wanted to win the Cup, but our momentum had come to a screeching halt. Because we are so competitive, we can become just as performance-driven and results-obsessed as any leader. We found ourselves frequently drifting back into horizontal thinking, replaying past races in our minds or getting anxious about the future.

But as we sat there at the banquet, our minds seemed to become re-centered. We were so proud of our guys for being nominated for an award that went far beyond performance. They didn't just volunteer in the community because we asked them to—they did it because they saw the deeper meaning of things. They did it because they were empathetic people. They did it because they had profound perspective. They did it because they were vertical thinkers.

Our moment of introspection gave way to a profound sense of accomplishment…thinking about the smiles on the children's faces as our guys chased them around the playground in a game of tag at a local elementary school…or how they humbly served lunch at the Charlotte Rescue Mission…or bolting together more than sixty children's bicycles, making our annual Race to the North Pole for the Ronald McDonald House the best year ever…or volunteering at charities of their own choosing throughout the year. The season did not produce the fairy-tale ending we would have scripted, but we had assembled an incredibly selfless group of people who became stalwarts in the community.

Though we knew we still had a long way to go in building what we wanted to build, being nominated for the award was a reminder to us that we were heading in the right direction. That our guys were developing perspective. That life was about much more than racing: it was about people. And that character and integrity were at the forefront of who we were. That we had indeed been successful.

And it was at that moment when Comcast executive Matt Lederer stood at the podium and announced our guys as the winner of the 2017 Comcast Community Champions Award. Winning the award was surreal. Over our combined years in NASCAR we had seen countless guys take their best shot at defeating Johnson and Keselowski, only to fall short. The unbelievable feeling of beating two of NASCAR's best was quickly made real by a $60,000 check that would be donated to the local Ronald McDonald House on our behalf, a nonprofit that provided room and board for suffering families traveling to the children's hospital to find the right type of medical help for their children. If you remember, our connection to the Ronald McDonald House had begun years before with our "Race to the North Pole" initiative, which management did not want us to pursue because they thought it'd be distracting.

If you are going to be a "less than ideal" listener, make sure you are willing to go down with the ship. However, we have found that you will be able to make it through stormy seas if your motives are rooted in two key values: one is hope, and the other is love.

9

Inspiring Great Efforts

The front and rear changers throw the old tires to the wall, switching the buttons on their air guns to "on" position. The jackman grabs the desired wheel spoke on the soon-to-be-installed new left-rear tire. A small spring on the side of the jack brings the handle to an upright and safe position. The carrier lifts the new tire preparing to install it on the left-front hub. The gasman empties gallons eleven through thirteen into the fuel cell.

-The 9th second of a NASCAR pit stop

You can no longer mandate great efforts! Great efforts can only be inspired. You cannot demand someone's very best! When leaders take the time to invest in their teams, it organically inspires great efforts on those teams. Inspiration is the predecessor to great efforts. Inspiration welds hope onto our hearts and minds, while mandating often shifts us into desperation. An important goal for all leaders is to inspire those they are leading to discover and reveal their best selves. It's up to leaders to commission this search.

So, what is one's best self? We've mentioned this term but have yet to define it. Simply put, it is the very best possible version of one's self. Your best self is the hardest-working version of you…the kindest version…the smartest version…the version that acts with the most integrity, etc. Some contemplative thinkers have called this the "true self"—the version of you that is not motivated by ego or status-related ambition and is instead motivated by love, selflessness, and servant leadership.

As with everything else, the search for your best self begins with your mindset. Each day, you move either toward the ideal version of yourself or away from it. Each day, it is not you versus your competition but rather you versus yourself. How can you improve from yesterday? What can you learn today that will help you tomorrow? How can you make someone else better today? What tough situations will you be in today that will make the "me" decision (the selfish decision) easy instead of the "we" (the selfless decision) decision? How can you make today meaningful and enjoyable for you and your coworkers or teammates? It's a leader's job to help people to develop this mindset and joyfully wrestle with these questions.

Within each person resides an unknown depth of power and gifts—incredible qualities and potential offerings to the world that many do not even know they possess. Often, the best self remains frozen inside a person because an environment is cold. Or a person is simply exhausted or burned out from the incessant pressure to perform. It is a societal norm to focus on deadlines, tasks, and quotas; we've been wired this way going all the way back to elementary school. When you are just a number in a massive organization, it is easy to focus tirelessly on tasks and deadlines. This is normalcy for lots of us, the highway of the status quo: masses in the congestive traffic of routines and processes stemming from the ideology of the Industrial Revolution that is now applied to how most corporations are run. The highest levels of exhaust exist in the greatest concentrations of traffic. Human beings are no different, and the exhaust is just as harmful. This corporate smog distracts us from fueling the personal growth and the flourishing of others.

Deadlines, like smog, allow you to see only what is directly in front of you. Solid leadership requires vision and faith to look beyond tasks, quotas, and deadlines. An underlying goal for leaders is for transformation to coincide with work, which requires that you inspire others to tap into the depths of their gifts. To help others find meaning in life, not just accomplishment. We try to send people on this journey, not only so they'll be the best teammates they can be, but also so they will be the best son, daughter, friend, spouse, and parent outside work.

Leaders, then, must embark on this journey themselves in order to send direction to those following them. We know that our group will not go on the journey to unleash their best selves if we ourselves are not going on that journey. We are committed to asking ourselves the hard questions. Personal growth and discipline are prerequisites that must be exercised daily for us to lead and serve in a way that is selfless.

We try to send those we are leading on this journey by praising the things we want to see. We attempt to fuel who they are over what they do. Whereas many leaders are just waiting to critique their employees for where they go wrong, we are looking to praise them for what they do well, especially things that have nothing to do with their performance in pitting race cars. For example, picking up a towel from the floor in the garage…or training a newcomer and helping him or her improve their skill set…or helping a teammate move to a new house or apartment on a day off. If our people are doing selfless, team-oriented things like that, we are confident that we can experience success against some of the most efficient human beings in the United States on pit road. But more than that, it gives us the confidence that we are all, together, becoming the grateful, humble, and selfless individuals we were made to be. We can be a rising tide. And a rising tide lifts all ships.

Consider this chapter a blueprint for inspiring this search for your best self every single day. By visiting the good, bad, and ugly of culture, you'll be reminded of what you can do to make *your* culture truly inspiring and brilliant. A place where others will want to go on the search for their best selves every day.

The 7/16-Inch Wrench

A story floats around NASCAR garages that illustrates this point of how *not* to inspire the search for the best self. It has become somewhat of NASCAR lore over the years of telling it. The story has taken on many iterations, but this is how one of the versions is told. It is our sport's shining example of how *not* to lead.

The story is about one of the big teams that had an unusually poor start to a season. The fifth race of the new season took the Series to Bristol Motor Speedway, and this team had not even cracked the top thirty in points. The mood in the race shop was one of desperation and hopelessness. When the green flag dropped that Sunday in Bristol, however, their car unexpectedly came to life. Their driver kept it in the top five all day long. But with just three laps remaining, the car blew a right-front tire and went careening into the wall. They went from running third to finishing thirty-seventh. Their day of promise was dashed.

Despite the lousy result, their run produced a great deal of optimism in their shop. They had shown that their cars were capable of running up front with the leaders. So it was to no one's surprise when a team meeting was called on the Monday immediately following the race. The prevailing thought among the mechanics was that the owner would use the strong run at Bristol to rally the people in the shop and help lift the attitude of the shop. They could not have been more wrong.

On that Monday morning, they all gathered in the middle of the shop floor, waiting to hear from the team owner. Like a king atop his throne, he stood in front of everyone, looking across the shop, and then produced a small wrench from his pocket. "I want everyone to listen," he started. "I want you all to know that each of you is worth the same to me as this 7/16-inch wrench."

The group was stunned, but the owner wasn't finished.

"And like this wrench, you each have a job to do. And like this wrench, each of you is just as replaceable. Now, get back to work."[10]

Happy Monday.

Not one employee left the meeting that day inspired to do his or her best work. How could they? We would even go so far as to say not one employee left that meeting wanting to do *any* type of work. Certainly not for an owner who spoke to them in that manner. Any semblance of hope or desire from their strong showing at Bristol was instead replaced by bitterness and disdain. Instead of being inspired, they were deflat-

---

[10]. The 7/16th-inch wrench speech mentioned in this book is one of three versions we've heard over the years. One of the other versions states that this speech wasn't made to his own team but was advice given to another team owner who had reached out for advice on how to run a successful race team. Interestingly, at the time this story spread through the garage, the team was just a few years out from winning the championship and had been contenders in recent years. Around that time, this owner's team was the most-funded team in NASCAR. A rule was made for this team specifically to limit the number of cars they could enter in a race any given weekend, at the complaint of other teams. They could have entered eight fully funded teams per race. Today they have two teams and have not cracked the top ten with either of those cars in more than a decade. It appears that they have had a small problem attracting some of the more talented, available people in the sport. Regardless of the conversation, its audience, or what version you've heard, if you are in racing, you know that story. And every story revolves around the statement that everyone is replaceable, like a 7/16-inch wrench.

ed. Instead of collaborating on how to turn good cars into great cars, many focused on finding new jobs. The owner shifted the attitudes, all right—in the wrong direction. That was a moment when he could have shifted his team from fifth gear to sixth, but he went from fifth to first. For our non-car readers, Google what this does to the motor when you have a few minutes. *Boom!*

Shifting culture has a lot of similarities to shifting gears. When thoughtfully sequenced from first gear to second to third to fourth to fifth to sixth, you gain horsepower and move forward. But if you recklessly grab gears, then in an instant, there is a puff of smoke, and you blow the motor.

The employees of that team processed the scene from that morning over and over and over again in their heads and among themselves. *One comment made by one person in power became a vacuum that sucked up all inspiration and deflated the human spirit.*

It didn't take long for the mechanics on other teams to hear the story, which only confirmed most people's suspicions about the owner and subtly let them know that they, too, were just as replaceable as a 7/16-inch wrench. When you're in a leadership position, your message reverberates far and wide. We work exceptionally hard to make sure our own people know that they are valued and have a lot to offer to their teammates and culture. Because the truth is that, when the 7/16 inch wrench incident occurred, no one that day felt valued by the person who was signing their paychecks.

The owner was obviously trying to leverage the fact that he was paying their salaries, but the reality is that most people would rather make less and feel valued for what they do than make more and be treated like they are worthless and replaceable. People succumb to a debilitating sense of hopelessness whenever leadership is done poorly. There's something about this kind of disrespect that goes directly against our inherent dignity as human beings. This approach also has direct implications on performance. This team was once the highest-funded, most-marketable team in racing. They had the most cars in the Cup Series and championship-caliber drivers, and they routinely found themselves in victory lane. Currently, it is the least-funded and has struggled to compete with the current giants of the industry. It has had a hard time retaining its top talent. We wonder why…

The Sweaty Man with a Heart of Gold

In NASCAR, most racing teams are named after the owner of the team, whose name is stitched onto uniforms, painted on cars, and plastered on the side of the team building. Though there's nothing wrong with this, seeing the owner's name everywhere is, sadly, all too often just an accurate reflection of the simple fact that the racing team is usually more about the owner than it is about the culture and all the good that culture can do. Much of the time, unfortunately, the owner's name is more of a representation of fear, frustration, and dread than it is pride and inspiration, as we saw in the last example.

Two-time Daytona 500 winner Michael Waltrip, however, was an exception to this narrative. When we worked at Michael Waltrip Racing (MWR), we were always struck by Michael's humility. He didn't act like he was better than you or higher up than you just because he was the one who was signing your paycheck. He knew all our names. He would always come outside while we were practicing and hang out with us, asking us questions about our families or passions outside of work. He brought a chaplain in every Tuesday for spiritual inspiration and bought lunch for all who attended. Whenever there was a problem with our performance, he would say things like, "Help me understand where we are going wrong" or, "What do you guys think the solution is?" He saw his employees as people who were more than machines, people who had much more of a role in his life than simply making him look good. He wanted to be with you, not boss you around. He wanted to listen and learn from you before telling you what to do. He would leave inspirational quotes and heartfelt messages on the whiteboard in the gym because he cared about his guys. MWR was an incredibly fun and inspiring place to work. Michael was one of us. We fought for him, literally, one year in the now-infamous Jeff Gordon vs. Clint Bowyer brawl in the garage at the Phoenix International Raceway. His team was our team.

Michael's raw humanity revealed how little he cared about his ego or perfected image. Sometimes he'd sleep in the shop and wake up to his employees arriving at work. He'd walk around in his pajamas and disheveled hair, talking to people, just being himself. Often, he would work out with our pit crew, and because he would sweat like crazy, everyone would hope he didn't show up to work out on a partner-stretch day because that usually entailed him putting his sweaty skin all over us as we stabilized him or held his leg. He didn't care. He saw himself as one of us, part of our group. He was a representation of us, even though his name was on the shirt.

Years later, after Michael had moved on from owning a racing team, we received the sad news that a mechanic who had worked at MWR for a few years and had spent his last few years at another racing team had tragically passed away in his sleep. However, it wasn't the mechanic's own racing team who stepped up to host his family during such a traumatic time—it was Michael Waltrip. Michael insisted that the memorial be hosted at his old racing headquarters.

In Michael's mind, he likely couldn't see the memorial being hosted anywhere else simply because of how he viewed his employees and former employees. He cared about his employees—and their families—like they were his own family. A banner proclaiming "Teamwork Makes the Dream Work" hung in his race shop for all to see. Michael knew that great efforts were best achieved together. He wanted success *with* the team, not *from* the team.

Life Moments Trump Business

Two characteristics that are absolute must-haves for leaders are selflessness and the ability to listen. One thing that served us well before we became coaches was to ask guys on other race teams what their organizations did well and where they might have missed the mark. We were amazed by what we heard—everything from coaches often being late to practice, to forty pit-stop practices the day after a bad race, to some coaches not even attending practice. We were hoping to learn what to do in these conversations, but we largely learned what not to do.

One of the more compelling complaints was from a young tire changer whose father was in what appeared to be a losing battle with cancer. His father's illness took a turn for the worse, and the family converged to support him and spend time with "Pops." The young tire changer left his race team to fly down to Florida to be with him at his bedside Thursday through Saturday, but then he had to fly up to Michigan for the race on Sunday. The reason he had to leave his ailing father? Because the race team he was working for wasn't going to pay him if he couldn't make it.

What if he had received a call at the track on Sunday from a family member telling him that his father had passed away? How would missing the final moments of his father's life to still get his paycheck (so he could continue to assist in taking care of a family member) inspire future efforts?

The first contract we wrote as head coaches included a provision that allowed up to two weeks of paid time off work for family emergencies or important life events. We didn't want someone who was at a family member's bedside to ever be thinking about work during those dense, poignant moments. We didn't want our guys missing their sister's wedding or the birth of a child or the last moments with a loved one. Moments like these are etched into our memories forever and are far more important to experience than anything we could ever do on a Sunday at the racetrack. If you have ever had the unfortunate privilege of sitting bedside with a beloved life that is on its final lap, the conversations are not about trophies or accomplishments. Rather, they are about the people who were a part of the race, the people who accompanied them on the journey.

As a leader, you can cultivate either an integrated culture or a compartmentalized culture. An *integrated* culture incorporates every single aspect of those you are leading—their unique personalities, their personal lives, and their needs. It integrates their spirit and soul, their heart and mind, their loved ones, and their deep passions. It is essentially seeing someone for the fullness of who they are. This fullness always extends far beyond the workplace.

A *compartmentalized* culture, on the other hand, treats those you are leading as robots—bodies for labor and ends to a means in the binary tunnel of achieving or underachieving. Compartmentalization creates a certain unawareness about people's situations and deeper needs. It satisfies the fundamental needs of shelter, food, and clothing through compensation but falls short of addressing the higher needs of authenticity, belonging, development, or fulfillment. It forces employees to create boundaries between them and leadership and daily objectives: to suppress who they are and to view the workplace as nothing more than a place to subsidize a life they wish they could spend more time in.

Could it be possible that empathy—elevating the humanity of every person and therefore their personal sufferings—taps into who we each innately are, cultivates togetherness, multiplies a deep sense of meaning on your team, integrates the personal with the professional, and ultimately inspires a more positive and efficient culture?

If you force your employees to miss those special moments, are you really going to get their best selves? Or will their professional lives begin to cause resentment within them? When people are resentful, are they going to positively impact your team's environment? Are they going to be 100 percent invested in the success of your team? Are they going to be efficient?

Our crews know that family comes first. Life moments trump business. And because we don't ask them to sacrifice life's most important moments for work, we don't obstruct opportunities for them to put their best foot forward at work. It's the give and take of high-performing teams. Cultural advantages occur in the mind. If a pit crew jumps off the wall and they are all thinking about lug nuts, wheel spoke patterns, etc., they have an advantage over a crew composed of people thinking about a significant life moment or the security of employment. Wholeness exists when people feel supported in their fears and worries. This wholeness leads to clarity. And clarity leads to focus. Seeing people in the fullness of who they are and all the wonderful parts of their lives opens the door to wholeness, clarity, and focus for individuals and for the entire team.

Aim for Impact

Information delivered without emotion goes unheard. While unchecked emotion acts as a thief, the emotions we do try to bring every day are the ones that fuel passion. One of our goals each day is that our guys will be able to see our passion for what we do, whether that is coaching them in a pit stop, interacting with people in different departments, playing Bump after practice, or planning a volunteering event. We want to be emotionally steady—even-keeled—but also consistent in demonstrating passion. We believe this can be done without getting overly angry or overly excited.

Passion is something that rises from a place that is deep within you, a place not casually accessible. People demonstrate consistent passion in the workplace whenever their job is an extension of their calling, whenever their job is an outlet to share the gifts they have to offer. We are passionate about genuine connection and creating high-functioning teams where a deep sense of meaning is experienced. Our job as coaches is an outlet for our gifts. We want to create a space that is an outlet for others' gifts as well so they can experience their calling in the workplace. This kind of passion is contagious and unmistakable.

Very rarely do you ever hear someone recommend a movie or show that is incredibly boring or uninspiring. Our guys can often be overheard quoting movies like *Remember the Titans, Fury, 300,* and *The Dark Knight Rises*. The reason they remember the lines well enough to repeat them is because they were inspired by the movies they came from. The movies that impact us the most are usually gripping stories that demand a personal and emotional response. Being a leader is like having an opportunity to direct a movie with those you are leading each and every day. The "movie" you create each day with your team can either invite others to be moved and inspired, or it can put them to sleep. Inspiring movies invite change and transformation, and they awaken something new within you. Passionate leaders open the gates for those they are leading to rally around a cause—a cause that stretches far beyond performance and actually taps into the things that are deeply meaningful to all people.

If your company met its goal of leading your industry in sales but took advantage of people, exploited people, and evaded taxes, is that "impact"? Congratulations on being on top of the industry, but this is a very shallow purpose. However, if you, as a leader, can say, "We underperformed a little bit this year, but we have happy people who love coming to work, our customers' engagement is great, and we made a dent as a team on child poverty," people can rally around that because it's something bigger than themselves. Connection is much deeper than sales. True impact has to be about people. Leaderboards are short term; purpose and meaning are lasting.

Culture done well leads to connection. Genuine relationships cultivate diversity of thought and uniqueness. Out of this uniqueness flows innovation, creativity, passion, and efficiency. So many company leaders believe they have a great product—and maybe they do—but they falsely think that people should buy it just because it's a great product. They advertise, for example, that they write the best mortgages in town.

Maybe they do have the best processes for doing so, but they hardly get to know their clients and are more interested in numbers than who those numbers represent. This is an example of people getting lost in a product or a process.

But consider companies like Apple and Chick-fil-A. Yes, they have great products. But what is it that makes the experience of that product special? Without question, it is their customer service. Something like Apple's "Genius Bar," where you can walk right in and schedule an appointment on the spot with customer care. Or the compassionate service you experience at the counter of every Chick-fil-A. Deep impact is often made when people are brought to the forefront of a company's mission—both their employees and those their employees serve.

For us, impacting people's lives is more than just turning someone into a better tire changer. Truly inspiring people isn't just about saying, "Let's beat this team!" or "Let's make this deadline!" or "Let's hit this quarterly goal!" It's about all the conversations, moments of connection, and memories you experience together along the way. It's about helping one another overcome situations in their personal lives that will help confidence and serenity overflow into their professional lives. Aiming for impact involves a much more holistic approach than simply focusing on a specific product or task. The best movies and shows just don't engage your eyes; they engage your heart and mind. Aiming for impact in the workplace doesn't just involve the hands and feet of people's labor; it involves engaging their hearts, minds, and cultivating that which makes them unique.

The After-Work Phone Call

Now that we've discussed how vertical thinking can inspire others to go on the search for their best selves, let's get a little bit more specific in highlighting some practical actions you can take routinely to inspire great efforts on your team. These kinds of things naturally flow out of vertical thinking and aiming for impact. But sometimes, it is helpful to have practical action points that you can either apply in your own leadership style or that inspire other similar ideas.

One strategy we try to implement throughout the season is the after-work phone call. Simple in its execution, yet profound in its impact, the after-work phone call is simply a phone call to those you work with that is made outside working hours. Its purpose is to let people know two primary things: one, how grateful you are for them and their efforts in the workplace; and two, how interested you are in their lives beyond the workplace. The purpose of this call is to get beyond the occasional post-work happy hour or organized team lunch and really show those you are leading that you see how valuable they are to you outside the workplace. It can really say a lot to a person when he or she gets a call from the boss, but the boss isn't asking for something that is work-related. It's sad, but most of us can count on one finger how many times a boss has called to say, "Thank you."

With all the pressures that exist in the workplace, a quick five-minute call that is focused on praise can go a long way in helping someone to feel empowered to take on the pressures and demands of their job. There is really nothing quite so invaluable as realizing that those who hired you or recruited you are for you and on your side. By noticing someone's efforts and validating who they are outside of work, you inspire them more than their paycheck ever could.

Names, Birthdays, Anniversaries, and Dinners

Another strategy we employ to show our guys that their lives matter to us is to invest in their personal lives and families. When they join our team, we ask them to fill out a form that asks for personal information. We want to know the names and birthdays of their spouses and their children. We want to know the dates of significant life events, like anniversaries and parents' birthdays. We put these dates in the calendars on our phones and have them set to remind us five minutes before we walk out to practice. It gives us the opportunity to mention these important dates to our guys when we see them out at practice that day. It shows we care, and it also helps us remind them of an important upcoming event, in case they forgot.

We ask a lot from our guys over the course of a thirty-nine-week NASCAR schedule. Helping them keep track of these life events might seem insignificant, but one would be incorrect with that assumption.

An example of its importance came one day when we were in our office at the end of the day reviewing film. One of our veteran guys walked up and said he had a couple things he wanted to work on but that he was close to finishing up for the day. He wanted our opinion of whether to stay and finish the project or if it was OK to resume in the morning. We responded by simply reminding him of his wife's birthday the next day. He immediately debated the point until the realization set in that he had forgotten. The look of horror on his face was unforgettable. Birthdays are a big deal in his family, and this particular guy was married to a lady affectionately known as "The Warden." Clearly, not someone you want to disappoint. We obviously won't name any names, but there have been several guys who have been so focused on work and tasks in the hustle and bustle of the NASCAR season that they completely forgot their anniversary, their dad's birthday, etc.

In doing these things, we make ourselves available to that person and his family, not only in the professional setting but also in a personal setting. Throughout each year, our pit crew members seek our advice about personal matters, whether it's buying a house or a car or managing a relationship or marriage. We ask a lot of our guys and routinely make things uncomfortable. Growth isn't forged in comfort but in fire. But, on the other side of the coin, we want our guys to know we are for them in every aspect of their lives, that we have their best interests in mind, and that we see them as more than a tire changer or a jackman or a fueler.

When we sign a new crew member, we often do it over dinner with the guy and his partner. On a few occasions, the spouses of veteran crew members stated that we were the only coaches who took time to get to know them. It meant a lot to them that we knew their names. Not only do we want our team members to feel valued; we want their families to know that we appreciate their sacrifices as well. When sacrifice goes unnoticed, it makes way for resentment. We want our guys' families to know that they are part of the team and that we couldn't do what we do without their support. Knowing their names, birthdays, anniversaries, and occasionally taking an employee and his/her partner out to dinner are simple, practical ways to show everyone involved in this chaotic industry that they have value.

Leading from the Middle

Your ability to impact others is bigger than you think. Too often, the tendency is to play small because of positioning within the company. But that is a lie we often tell ourselves.

You can lead from the middle right now.

Consider your company a circle with "the middle" being equidistant from every end point within the company or everyone within your culture in the company. Leading from the middle is about being approachable and reliable, not only with work issues but also with personal issues. People bring their personal lives into work, so it makes sense to understand each person on a deep, personal level. Leading from the middle is also about seeing things non-hierarchically. It's about crossing the threshold. When we are in front, it fuels our ego, and we leave guys behind. When we are in the back, we miss out on the fight, and lose touch with the journey. We've found it best to be in the middle.

We don't just do this with our pit crews. It extends beyond our department. We also want those whose paths we cross each day know that we are available and approachable. We try to know every person's name in our 200-person company. For some, this might be unrealistic, so maybe it's best to start with knowing everyone in your department. If you're an executive in a company with a couple hundred people, you should definitely know every person's name because you're paying them. Many higher-ups don't realize how far it would go within their own company if they were just more available and visible within every corner of the company.

One simple strategy to create connection is parking on a different side of the building each day and taking a different route to your office. We do this so that we have to walk through a different part of the racing team headquarters and interact with different people. One day, we'll go through the assembly area…the next day the fab shop…the next day the truck bay…and so on. We ask our guys to do this, too, and they find it very fulfilling, as do we, because of all the different people we get to talk to and experience along the way.

If you're the president of a company and you had five conversations with five different people a day, it would take only fifty days to foster 250 unique interactions. And it's basically effortless. The beauty of this, too, is that when you make it a priority to get to know someone, you will find yourself thanking them and serving them. It brings humanity back into the workplace.

Often, when we speak to company leaders about their culture, we ask them, "Can you give us the name of one of your janitors?" Most of the time, people look at us dumbfounded because they have no idea. Usually, out of embarrassment, they will counter and tell us that they know their janitors' names only because they were preparing for this question. Every single guy in our program not only personally knows our janitors but will go out of their way to say hello, bump fists, or shake their hands. And every bit of it is authentic. Heck, our guys even attempted to teach one of our young janitors how to change tires!

A quick way to evaluate your environment is by how you treat the people at the bottom of the hierarchical structure, not how you take care of your executives. It's interesting that if a large company is missing one of its accountants for a week, people might not notice, but if it's missing a janitor for a week or if the toilet in the bathroom is broken because the janitorial staff is understaffed, everyone will notice it. The notion of mutual respect and connection among all employees of a company has gotten lost in hierarchy. Leading from the middle ignites dignity. If you are a higher-up in a company but don't know the names of people who you would view to be at the very bottom, then you probably aren't an impactful leader—you certainly aren't leading from the middle.

A great example of the power of subtle leadership, not surprisingly, comes from Rick Hendrick, the most accomplished team owner in NASCAR motorsports. The pit crew of one of his teams was sitting at the bar of the team hotel having a beer the day before a big race when suddenly the Big Boss appeared. The guys immediately quieted down to let Mr. H know they weren't out of control but just winding down for the evening and very much focused on the race for the next day. To their surprise, Mr. H said he really appreciated the hard work they had been putting in, that they were a huge part of their company, and that he was very proud of them. He then told the bartender that they could eat or drink whatever they wanted for the rest of the night. "Put it on my tab," he said.

This is impressive for several reasons. The first is that Mr. H. was staying at the same hotel as the team, which is incredibly rare. The second is that he knew who his guys were outside of team apparel. We've been on several teams where our president or owner walked right by us without acknowledgment (even when we spoke to them) because we weren't wearing team-branded gear, and they apparently had no idea who we were. The third is that of the four pit crews at Hendrick Motorsports at that time, this one was the poorest-performing. Human connection was still just as important to Mr. H. Human connection inspires performance.

A common mistake company leaders make when trying to reshape their culture is that they need millions of dollars to do so. We hardly ever think that is necessary. Mr. H understood that money can't replace presence. Availability is key. And, it's easy to let people know you're available. Interact with new people each day. Park in a different parking spot. Know everyone's name, and it's OK to ask if you don't. People will forget that you didn't know or remember their name if you are genuinely grateful for them and take time to listen to them.

Again, it is the unexpected gestures that people remember. People expect a check every few weeks. They are not expecting a phone call or a thank you or a conversation about raising kids. You can really catch people off-guard by acknowledging the important moments in their own lives and reaffirming that you care about them and who they are beyond the workplace. It's simple. It's free. It's profound. And most importantly, it cultivates connection.

Leading from the middle is about doing the small things with pride and intention. Sadly, the reality is that many people these days are willing to do things like helping teammates after work or cleaning a workstation that isn't their responsibility only if there is something in it for them. Just about everything in our society has become transactional for financial or social advancement. By leading from the middle, you can bypass the hierarchical workplace clutter and really start to develop a tight-knit, meaningful culture that is animated by inspiration.

Great efforts are successful efforts. According to Benjamin Franklin, the blueprint for success is trying, and trying again, until you are successful. However, trying ≠ success. Trying + learning + growing + inspiration + trying = success. You, as a leader, have an important role to play in the success of the individual and the organization. Your ability to inspire is 20 percent of the formula. Great efforts are waiting on you.

10

P = W/T

The front changer moves his left knee inward to create space for the new tire while eyeing his first lug nut. The jackman, tire in hand, slams the tire into the wheel opening, choosing the wheel stud pattern mid-flight (for example, "12 o'clock" or "snake eyes"). The carrier firmly holds the tire to the car to maximize lug nut torque. The rear changer passes the old left-rear tire to the gasman while switching the button on his air gun to the "on" position. The gasman prepares to kick the old left-rear tire to an awaiting tire catcher behind the wall while pouring gallons thirteen through fifteen.

-The 10th second of a NASCAR pit stop

Speed is the new currency of business. Rupert Murdoch is on record as saying that, "It is no longer big business versus small business. It is fast business versus slow." As the pace of life continues to accelerate, companies continue to develop processes in an attempt to stay ahead of the curve. But efficiency within a company is much more than simply streamlining a process.

What is often forgotten is that it is *people* who have to put those processes into motion. If you want a more efficient environment, people must be elevated over processes. This will foster communication, connection, and camaraderie, which help processes run more smoothly and are key components to efficiency.

P=W/T stands for *power equals work over time*. We have a department of employees…of people…of potential leaders who can unleash their best selves and influence the collective choices of the group. We give our crews a body of work to tackle, and once they complete that work, we want them out of the building and on their way home to their families and the other parts of their lives.

Throughout the racing industry, specifically NASCAR, the workplace is fraught with managers who hold an antiquated ideology that your value is determined more by the hours you clock rather than by what you get accomplished while you are working. But a hard-working employee isn't necessarily hard-working just because he or she is the first one there and the last one to leave. Those are incredible allies for your success but that doesn't necessarily make that person dedicated or efficient. Just as good management may not always lead to good leadership, quantity doesn't always lead to quality. We know a guy who quickly shot through the ranks at Wells Fargo by goofing off most of the day and starting his work at five o'clock in the evening when everyone left to go home. His bosses assumed that he was incredibly dedicated to the success of the organization as he led the departments in overtime month after month.

The better our crews can navigate the challenges of the day and the more efficient they can be, the sooner they can go home. What we want is people going after their work with full intention. And if they complete what we think is going to be a three-week project in two weeks, then we are fine with giving them a week off. This inspires efficiency and innovation rather than enslaving them to a formulaic clocking of hours.

We can't tell you how many conversations we've had with people in office jobs in other industries who can knock the heart of their work out in three hours but then spend over half of their day wasting time playing a game or scrolling through social media because they're trapped in their cubicle or office. The alternative is to take a longer route to complete *xyz* so that it passes the time. It's insane. But when the most important thing to bosses is that their employees stick to a schedule or get to work on time and stay until five o'clock to fulfill required hours, can you necessarily blame an employee for intentionally being inefficient? They are just playing by the rules of the game.

Another common thing we hear is people saying something along the lines of, "My bosses make me _____, but it'd be so much easier and better if we did it _____." A lot of employees in larger companies who we talk to feel handcuffed because they don't have the freedom to take a more innovative route. Their company's emphasis on "how we've always done it"—tradition—blocks their creative freedom. Not all traditions are healthy. Employees consequently become frustrated with their bosses, suppress their creativity, and ultimately are turned from human beings—with forward thoughts and ideas—to robots, simply there to complete a task; and not only to complete a task but to complete a task in a very specific way. One of the great tragedies in workplaces everywhere is that great ideas often go unheard. The truth is that every organization in the world has someone on their team right now who could help their company be more efficient.

Power is another one of those concepts that can multiply itself endlessly. It has increasing depth. Our pit crew members know when they come to work that it's time to dive in fully and apply every aspect of themselves—their bodies, hearts, and minds. There is no point in not giving their all because anything that is lacking in their effort is only going to make their workday longer and more difficult. So, they tackle their work with intention and full presence. Then, the next day they try to improve upon the day before. And so forth. Their processes continue to improve and become more efficient based on their past experience and desire to complete their work better. They might be working fewer hours at times but are working with more efficiency, innovation, and passion.

When people dedicate all of themselves to the work they have to do and focus on the task instead of the clock, they will naturally want to come up with ways to be more efficient and effective because they'll be rewarded with more time and freedom. Keeping people trapped in an office until a specific time isn't an inspired workplace. Rewarding people for applying all of themselves will inspire them to think outside the box, refrain from coasting, and be fully present.

Our job as coaches is not about clocking hours to collect a paycheck. It's not about making sure that those above us think favorably of us. Our job is about leading people and developing leaders. Our job is helping each of our guys to cultivate the best version of themselves. Which leads to diversity of thought. Which leads to efficiency. This *kind* of efficiency is power.

Economy of Movement

When you're trying to change four tires and fuel a car in 12 seconds, every single movement matters. During practice, we record video of every pit stop and gather around a screen afterward to dissect the efficiency of each person's movement and fundamentals. We will spend months trying to shave away microscopic, wasted movements that our guys make—an unneeded step, an angling of the wrist, a lowering of the shoulders.

The improvements we make equate to fractions of time and fractions of movement. If a pit stop consists of 160 total movements, then we know we can cut down our time consistently by somehow trying to chip away at those movements, slowly but surely—from 160 to 157, from 157 to 155, from 155 to 154, and so on—just to cut off two-tenths of a second. But as we've mentioned several times, that-two tenths of a second can be the difference in $1.1 million in earnings.

We see everything in movements. The economy of movement is the breakdown of your work over time. If 160 movements results in a twelve-second pit stop, then we need to figure out how to make fewer movements in less time to create a more powerful outcome. We don't focus on time. We focus on movement and movement fundamentals. When you eliminate unnecessary movement, you save time.

There's economy of movement in the workplace, too. We notice employees who work on the other side of the building who will pass three bathrooms on their way to a specific one. We will go to a coffee shop and notice the inconvenient location of certain equipment, causing employees to get in each other's ways.

Processes that are in place that will lead to more power should not be rushed. In analyzing movements as young coaches, we made the mistake of making urgency the main course—*speed* was all that mattered. The main course now is movement economy. Urgency is a side dish. Urgency should not take the place of that which is important, that which can be powerful. It is rarely a "sprint" to develop an efficient culture or minimize movements. It is, also, not a marathon. It is rather a relay in which individuals, teams, and departments work cohesively with uncommon skill, adeptness and proficiency. The secret is patience and the focus is daily, incremental improvement over time. Usain Bolt runs with urgency. He has to. He is a sprinter, and speed is all that matters. Lebron James, however, is unquestionably powerful. He runs with speed and strength. Powerful companies, like athletes, are the ones that have sustainable speed and strength.

Investing Time

What is time? What role does it serve in the workplace? Does it represent crisis or opportunity or both? And, what separates those who manage time wisely vs. those who do not? If gratitude is the currency of fulfillment, perspective is the currency of those who manage time wisely. We can take this even further and examine the way a leader references time.

For example, going back to the parable about the three people who were laying bricks, someone who sees work as a *job* finds himself or herself *killing* time; someone who sees work as a career believes he or she is *sacrificing* time; but someone who sees work as a *calling* will *invest* time.

"I'm just killing time trying to get to the end of the day," is a workplace phrase uttered by someone devoid of both passion and purpose. Time is one of the only resources that we have that is finite. We cannot manufacture time or buy any more of it. Someone who admits that they are wasting it to conclude their day is not a leader. When two-tenths of a second holds as much value to us as it does, there is no excuse to ever waste a second.

A *good* leader might take the time to do extra work for his or her team but wrongly believes that it's a sacrifice. A person like this might stay late so that everyone else can leave at the regular time or work on weekends so that everyone else can keep their weekday schedule, but then that person is going to let his or her team know about the sacrifice that was made. "I guess I don't mind sacrificing my time if it benefits the team." This disposition is transactional leadership. There's a certain martyrdom that comes with sacrificing time that does not lend itself to selflessness or servant leadership.

A *great leader*, however, takes the time to do the same things that a good leader does but has a completely different posture of the heart. A great leader operates under a banner of selflessness. A great leader never feels like his or her effort or energy is sacrifice. It's an investment that is in everyone's best interest. "I am going to invest my time with the developmental tire changers because they could prove to be the future of our pit crew."

Killing time. Sacrificing time. Investing time. The manner in which you reference time and approach the concept of time speaks volumes about you as a leader.

Everyone experiences challenges in the workplace, but these difficulties have less impact on the one who is enjoying the moment than the one who is at work purely out of obligation. Investing time into a calling—a purposeful meaning of existence—is enjoyable. People tend to be competent and successful at what they enjoy. This brings us back to our opening equation. The lens in which we view our "work" is more important than we think. Perspective concentrates, empowers time.

The Six Best vs. the Best Six

In the off-season that followed a breakthrough season for our pit crew, we lost four out of our six starters for our top car. To lose 66 percent of our top-performing team was a significant loss—the equivalent of an NBA team losing the majority of its starters after a solid playoff season or a baseball team having to replace its entire infield.

Our starters that year had mostly consisted of athletes who other race teams had passed on, but their stellar team performance now captured the attention of other race teams on pit row. In the offseason, the lure of substantially more money led two of them to not renew contracts with our team. What shocked people in our own organization the most was that after losing these two guys, we allowed a couple other guys to get out of their contracts, freeing them to make the same choice as their previous teammates.

Deciding to release these two guys led to us being questioned by just about everyone in our organization. Executives. Mechanics. The crew chief. Why would we *willingly* let two starters go after losing two of our starters to other racing teams? The reason, however, is because we were looking for the *best six* starters, not the six best.

Most people attempting to assemble a high-functioning team start out by trying to recruit and hire the six best people—the six most talented individuals—not the best six people, the most *effective* team. The best six are the ones who might not necessarily have the most talent individually but have the best opportunity to form a collective identity, move culture forward, and transcend talent with connection.

And that's exactly what they did.

Our guys united around each other, rallied around a team mantra, and developed a noticeable synergy that out-rivaled every other pit crew with more talent, resources, and time-together. They won the Mechanix Wear Award for outstanding pit crew for the first quarter of the season right out of the gate, dominating the field the first ten races. They were a finalist for Pit Crew of the Year.

There are no bigger incubators of human emotion than *team environments*. Unity creates an identity that can be a competitive advantage. We might have lost four of our starters. We might not have had the six best in the field on paper. But our men gelled and became the best six when there were many reasons why they should not have. They were intrinsically motivated and had a collective energy that instantly clicked. Because of their togetherness, our culture was strengthened in a way that never would have been possible had we tried to hold onto the guys that weren't 100% in, though they were incredibly talented. These decisions take courage. It also takes courage to place the team above self. Doing this fosters unified group identity, and unified groups yield powerful results.

Togetherness

An old African proverb states, "If you want to go fast, go alone. But if you want to go far, go together." We knew from the beginning, when we took over as pit crew coaches, that our cohesiveness as a unit would be our greatest strength. We created a list of "non-negotiables." A list of behaviors we felt could be so destructive to our culture and that would not be tolerated in any situation. And we were hypervigilant making sure that they did not show up.

An example of this came during our first year from our third pit stop in the Federated Autoparts 400 when our rear tire carrier badly missed his index, losing us valuable seconds. As soon as the jack dropped and the car accelerated out of the pit box, our front tire carrier threw his hands in the air and screamed, "Dammit!" expressing his displeasure for the costly mistake. By doing this he put himself above the team trying to absolve himself of the mistake through his theatrics. We immediately stepped into that moment. "If you ever throw one of your teammates under the bus like that again, it'll be your last race here!" I (Peet) yelled, nose to nose amid the deafening roar of the race.

It was the only time either of us has ever screamed at one of our guys in the middle of the race, but it was necessary for the preservation and cultivation of our relationship-centered culture. It didn't matter that this person happened to one of the most talented and highest-paid athletes on our team—we were serious about cutting him if he didn't change his attitude and the way he responded to team members when things weren't going well. If you are only a good teammate when things are going well, you aren't a good teammate. What you love, you protect. We love our guys and the space we all work in. To not protect the space in that moment would be unloving.

Your culture is only as strong as the worst behavior you tolerate. We knew that individualism and finger pointing would not lead us or our culture anywhere we wanted to go, and it was important to minimize these moments when and if they ever showed up. Someone's ego and selfishness was on full-display, and it was up to us to make sure from the start that a disposition like that wouldn't be tolerated. Those attitudes are a cancer to creating a united identity. As a leader, it's up to you to recruit people who aren't going to be controlled by their egos, the kinds of people who will be resentful or self-absorbed. And it's also up to you to position your team to form this bigger identity.

Similarly, whereas most pit crew coaches practice each of their teams separately throughout the week, from their top-ranked crew to bottom-ranked crew, all of our pit crew members practice together. We are probably one of the only teams in NASCAR that practices like that. Everything we do, we do together. The reason we approach practice like this is because it allows everyone to put sweat on the floor at the same time and for each person to witness the sacrifice and hard work of others. That's the togetherness piece that really binds us. Suffering through workouts together brings us closer and closer. Whether you are a starter on our top pit crew or someone who is fighting for a spot, each person has a role, and no one is more important than the next.

Even when we do break up into teams for, say, lift days, it's not by rank or performance. Throughout much of the year, it's position-based—our jackmen, gasmen, and tire changers/ carriers practicing together and zeroing in on exercises that build strength for their particular roles. Later in the year, we often group people together for lift days based on injuries and ailments. So we will have a "bad back" group or "bad knee" group or "hip problem" group, working in unison in order to build strength together. It's never performance-based or hierarchical. We never want anyone to feel alienated or on the outside looking in because of their performance on the race track. Rather, we want their togetherness to create inspiration, which we believe will ultimately positively influence their performance.

Separating pit crew members based on their performance or rank is the American workplace's equivalent of the higher-ups working in offices and everyone else working in cubicles. It took no longer than a week at our new job for us to rip the sign off of our office which read, "Mike Metcalf and Shaun Peet, Pit Crew Coaches." We have an office area upstairs with the rest of the "higher-ups" or "carpet-walkers" but we don't keep our belongings there and rarely work there. We, in our own accord, moved into a tiny office we occupy together that is close to the pit practice prep area and training room. We did this because, one, it's more efficient—it's where we spend most of our time; and, two, we didn't want our guys to feel that there is any hierarchical separation between us and them. We were metaphorically knocking down the walls, as a number of large companies are doing, and turning our work environment into a co-working space where collaboration and togetherness can thrive.

Death Metal on Race Day

Runaway emotions are a thief. They rob you of your clarity of thought. They rob you of your efficiency. And they can rob you of respect. If you don't have reign over your own emotions, you don't provide those you lead with any type of foundation.

Emotional efficiency, however, isn't about suppressing your emotions—it's about having control over them. Processing them is the key; *not* constantly reacting to them. Instead, you receive them, evaluate them, deal with them, confront them, and simultaneously keep moving forward in a way that they do not derail you. In our "outrage society" we are very quick to react to something said or done to us. We treat our emotions as directives rather than suggestions, and this can often lead us down the wrong path. Just because someone's words or actions evoke a feeling in us does not mean that we must act on it. Viktor Frankl stated, "Between stimulus and response there is a space. In that space is our power to choose our response. In our response lies growth and our freedom." People that manage their emotions well are able to simply allow the stimulus to inform them so that they can come up with the best way to proceed forward.

Runaway emotions are not always related to something negative. Once, for example, we had a guy whose fundamentals were always sound during practice but he always seemed to lose a step on race day and make mistakes that he hardly ever made throughout the week. Race days are emotionally intense already—high-pressure and high-stress, not to mention the sensory overload that comes with fighter jets blazing over the track, the car engines roaring, all the sights and the smells in that hyperactive space, and crew chiefs constantly reminding you that the next stop is really important so "try not to suck." Still, our guy was a tenured crew member, we knew he was used to the intensity of race day, and we still couldn't figure out the solution.

However, during the delay between the national anthem and the grand Marshall instructing the drivers to start their engines, we noticed that he had his headphones on. One of us approached him and asked if we could take a listen. It was intense, industrial death metal best described as musical insanity. He was using that type of music to get emotionally amped up for the upcoming race. We asked him how that served to benefit his efficiency and when he couldn't answer we told him that he could no longer listen to that type of music anymore. His presence of mind would serve him better than the untethered adrenaline being produced by his musical selection.

These kinds of emotions might serve guys well before they take the football field, but it doesn't serve us well. It doesn't serve most people well in the workplace. Getting "psyched" before a big moment where performance matters is usually more detrimental than beneficial. There's a real difference between passion and intensity. You can be level-headed and composed and still be passionate. Most people are turned off by intensity as is your clarity of thought and with it, your sound fundamentals. These kinds of heightened emotions cloud judgment. In pitting race cars, we don't want death metal. We want Jack Johnson.

Just like the first story, this young man's efficiency was affected by his runaway emotions. Fundamentals and level-headedness can get lost in any kind of heightened emotion that is not controlled, whether it be anger, excitement, or sadness. Efficiently managing your emotions is a precursor to optimal performance.

Efficient Communication

Managing your emotions and not letting them derail you is an internal process. But when it comes to helping the team, the external manifestation of the internal, communication is key. If you want to put Power = Work/Time (P=W/T) into motion on a collective level, it all boils down to communication.

We know we have to be expert communicators to have a chance at success. We have had races where a tire blew out in Turn 4, and we were pitted close to the entrance of pit row. The fuel window and strategy is to pit in ten laps, but suddenly the car is in the pit stall. You have to act instantly. You have to be able to give your teammate a certain look or hand gesture, and your teammate has to understand exactly what you're communicating…without saying anything at all. That's the beauty of creating a culture where relationships are of utmost importance. This return to elevating human connection above everything else ultimately benefits the work that we do. The depth of our relationships creates an intimacy, transparency, and understanding that really benefits us in high-pressure situations.

Also, because relationships are most important in our culture, our guys want to deal with any residual conflict or tension. They want to communicate with one another and navigate the different struggles that naturally arise. How many times in the workplace do people just dance around the periphery of what they really want to say? How often has an unattended matter truly resolved itself? How many times have you been in a long meeting where the purpose of the meeting isn't communicated until the fiftieth minute because those who are leading the meeting are unprepared or afraid to bring up the conflict, tension, or challenge? It's not efficient at all to have meetings that can be done in five minutes but take an hour. But people either fear confrontation or they like to hear themselves talk, which is all tied up in the ego. They think that the longer they hold the floor, the more depth it gives to their idea, but the truth is that a good idea is a good idea. Present it, let it live on its own, and if it's good, it'll take flight. Merry-go-round meetings are not efficient forms of communication, yet they happen all the time.

We love the teams that use formulas for their meetings or brainstorming sessions similar to this: submit, report, discuss, and suggest. Submit your report beforehand so that no one is caught off guard with content and that everyone is prepared for discussion. Is there something to report? If so, report it succinctly. Is there anything that needs to be discussed based on what was reported? If so, discuss it with intention, not just to hear yourself talk. And finally, is there something that needs to be acted upon based on what was reported and discussed? If so, clearly suggest action items with solutions and options, and then move on. This process saves time and eliminates unnecessary conversation.

Merry-go-round meetings are an example of inefficiency because very little meaningful work is getting done in a large amount of time. Participants just keep reiterating and rehashing the same point over and over again. It is nothing short of maddening. If you want your team to collectively get the best work done in a small amount of time, communication is key. Healthy communication will naturally arise out of relationship-focused environments.

Process Improvement

Process is defined as *a series of actions or steps taken to achieve a particular end*. Our process improvement sees us searching out and carving off tenths of seconds from unnecessary movements.

NASCAR pit stops are a model of process improvement. When pit stops were in excess of one minute, the Wood brothers came up with a hydraulic jack that lifted the car in one stroke, replacing the old floor jack that took a dozen strokes to lift the car. Pit stops dropped to forty seconds. Next, tire changers started gluing lug nuts onto the wheels instead of installing each one by hand. Pit stops dropped to twenty seconds. Then, teams started staffing their pit crews with football, baseball, and hockey players and used their explosive athletic ability to drop pit stops into the twelve-second range. Teams started investing millions of dollars into pit gun development and the first sub-ten-second pit stop was executed. These were huge leaps in process improvement over the course of fifty years of racing.

Process improvements are limited not mainly from an inability to update a process but rather challenges in updating assets, re-training employees, or updated implementation. Process Improvement sounds good until you have to do it. However, we have found that people are not afraid of change. Their fear lies in the unknown that often accompanies change. The concern lies in the unscripted consequences that change inevitably invites. Script the consequences and prepare to amaze yourself.

For example, in 2018, we settled on a choreography for pit stops that best suited our organization. We adjust our cars a lot, which means placing a wrench in the rear glass of the car during a pit stop and turning a plate on top of the springs up or down to adjust the feel of the car. Some of the teams we compete with will go races without making adjustments. We adjusted ours during almost every stop. To start 2019, we decided to abandon the adjustment-friendly choreography (with the tire carrier starting from the rear of the car) to go with the overall faster style of having the tire carrier attack from the front of the car. There was only one problem: How would we adjust the car?

Within a week, we had it solved. New wrenches were made, mouthguards were purchased, and adjustments were happening again, but this time, faster. The tire carriers running out into traffic with sixty-five-pound tires in each hand would carry the wrench out, in their mouths. What is our process to improving process?

1. *Look*. Look around and see what successes others (individuals or business) are having around you. Gather ideas, and create a baseline.
2. *Dream*. Create a dream process. Think vertically. How could you do this if money or time was of no concern? What would you do if you had nothing to inhibit you from daring thinking?
3. *Collaborate*. What would be the most efficient and economical way to implement this dream scenario? Get others involved in

this conversation so that it becomes a cross-departmental initiative. People like challenges. Observe toddlers; problem solving is primal. Collaboration challenges the team while simultaneously increasing accountability.
4. *Count.* The costs, that is. Make a plan and budget time and money. And count every small failure along the way. Efficiency often has more to do with continuously minimizing failures over time more so than quickly arriving at successes.
5. *Start.* There is never a good time to begin a new project. Never a good time to overhaul a system that is working, even if it is working poorly. Efficiency doesn't wait for a truck stop for our truck drivers to switch drivers on long trips to/from racetracks. They switch while the truck is in motion. True story. Get moving! The smallest action trumps the grandest intention.
6. *Design.* Create a wrench, a software, a system, a plan, an ad-hoc committee, a task force, a team, or a process with the implementation of the process as the destination, not the process itself. One of our starting tire carriers suggested we carry it via mouth, our pit technical lead drew up a new wrench with one of our backup tire carriers, another tire carrier got mouth guards that could grip the wrench for all the guys at his position, a fabricator welded a prototype wrench together, and we were off and running, practicing as if this was the way that we had always done it.
7. *Embrace.* Embrace for impact; there may be a wreck or ten as the process unfolds. Plan for that and shift resources to cover any shortcomings that may occur. Embrace is also a synonym for hugging, coming together. Stick together when turbulence hits. It is calculated turbulence that facilitates flight.
8. *Endure.* This is the most vital part. You're close to doing something the industry has never seen, something no one else is doing but everyone needs. You're writing a song that someone needs to sing. Today's comforts are the enemy of tomorrow's greatness. Don't give up.
9. *Speak.* Talk about the success of your new process, even if it hasn't happened yet. Speak positively about how this change is good and going to work. Words are things, our words have more power than we think. Fuel your faith, not your doubts.

10. *Birth*. Unveil your new process with confidence, knowing there was underlying intention all along the way. You will be the new standard.
11. *Celebrate*. Celebrate the failures, the successes, and all the lessons on this PI journey. Also, a handshake and sincere thank you to all involved is appropriate.
12. *Repeat*. Start over, improving on your improvements, when necessary.

What process-improvement journey do you need to start today?

Everything Matters

The changers hit the fourth of five lug nuts on the new left-side tires. The jackman shifts back to the jack handle. The carrier shifts to the nose of the car. The gasman fills the car up to seventeen and a half gallons.

-The 11th second of a NASCAR pit stop

True success doesn't reward the wrong organization. If you want to experience championship moments, every single detail has to matter. We know we cannot perform a 12-second pit stop without being intentional about every tiny detail of all that goes into every second of a pit stop: each person's mindset, emotions, economy of movement, fundamentals, and the chemistry and communication among teammates.

When that car speeds into the pits for the first time on race day, we know that each second of our pit stop is much more than a good second or a bad second, an efficient second or a second that falls short of a desired outcome. Each second is a culmination of our culture. It is born out of an intentional congruence that is woven through everything we've done as a team throughout the week—mentally, emotionally, and physically—along with everything we've done the past several years to bolster our environment. Each second is a mini-film of collective choices. Each second is loaded with meaning.

In NASCAR racing, the importance of each physical movement of every pit crew member, in each second of a pit stop, is on full display for thousands of viewers to see. It is a stark reminder that even the smallest detail is of the utmost importance. But the truth is that every little movement matters, no matter your industry. Performance might be what most choose to focus on, but within performance, whether it is good or bad, is a culmination of moments. Success, over time, ultimately comes from being intentional in everything you do. Just as the difference in two-tenths of a second can determine who wins a race, the smallest issue, conflict, or haphazard communication can have massive consequences in your workplace or culture.

Bringing intention sharpens attention to the smallest details—each conversation; each movement in every process; and each person's personality, mentality, dreams, and goals. Opportunities to move the needle for your company are everywhere. True leaders realize that every minuscule detail in the makeup of their team and in each moment of every day is an opportunity to strengthen culture. Consistent incremental improvement over time is the secret of high-functioning teams.

When it comes to culture—which is the only thing that will sustainably move your team, department, or company forward consistently over a long period of time—everything matters.

Creating Intention

William A. Foster, a United States Marine in the 3rd Battalion, 1st Marines, once said, "Quality is never an accident; it is always the result of high intention, sincere effort, intelligent direction, and skillful execution. It represents the wise choice of many alternatives."

Moments on the championship stage begin with intention. It's up to leaders to create intention in establishing culture and implementing those principles on a day-to-day level. In *The Cubs Way: The Zen of Building the Best Team in Baseball and Breaking the Curse*, President of Baseball Operations Theo Epstein put together a "player development manual" that would eventually provide the bedrock principles for the 2016 World Series champion Chicago Cubs, after a 108-year championship drought. Leadership tried to commit to these cultural tenets each day in how they led the Cubs organization and inspired their players and employees to unleash their best selves. In the manual are six key principles:

1. We will treat the development of every player as if we are making a personal investment in him.
2. We will stay objective in evaluating the player's strengths and weaknesses in order to devise the most precise and thorough individual player development plan.
3. We will continually challenge ourselves to better communicate our method of teaching.
4. We will always put the organization's goals ahead of our personal ambition.
5. We will embrace the cultures and backgrounds of all of our players, foreign and domestic, as we recognize the growth we can achieve as an organization from this experience.
6. At all times, we will keep this in mind: our mission is to help the Chicago Cubs win a world championship!

The Cubs players bought into this so entirely that whenever one of these behaviors showed itself on the field or in the clubhouse, the players would recognize it by saying, "That's Cub"—an affirmation that the player was holding himself to the values the club deemed essential to winning a championship. Again, you do not have a high-functioning culture when you as the leader have to *enforce* championship behavior. You have a high-functioning culture when players on your team hold each other to the standard you have set.

Our key principle when we first began coaching was that we were going to win with good people. We have tried to base every significant decision we've ever made around this principle. Our men know that we place tremendous value on character and work ethic. As for winning, we aim to create a culture of excellence through daily competition.

There's a common understanding by everyone in our culture that we are going to compete at everything we do to replicate the intensity of race day. Competition is integral in our daily environment. If there is the opportunity to go head to head at anything, our guys are game. And regardless if it's pit stops or ping-pong, successful outcomes lead to bragging rights and are thus highly coveted.

Our most competitive day is Wednesday—the day of the week that is equidistant between the past race and the next race. We never want to get too far removed from the intensity of what we feel on weekends. In an attempt to replicate the pressure that is felt on the racetrack, we will, for example, put pressure on a tire changer by having everyone on the team place bets on how many lug nuts he'll hit on a practice pit stop, and whoever guesses incorrectly pays his penance with a run up the hill. A scenario like this organically creates a pressure-filled scenario. As the kid is changing lug nuts, everyone is crowded around the car, watching his every move, either cheering him on or heckling him, not wanting to be in the group that has to run a mile. How much more mentally prepared is that tire changer going to be on the intensity of race day when he is used to having all eyes on him?

We also stage competitions in the weight room and during workouts. We routinely pit teams against one another, with nothing riding on the outcome other than pride. It can get pretty intense sometimes—and we'd be lying if we said there were never heated moments. But because these moments consist of high-character people, our guys know that our togetherness and unity is the bottom line. Our togetherness can bend at times, but our collective success demands that we never break. Our togetherness, in fact, is what makes space for all the competition to exist. As we mentioned, whereas most racing teams have their starters practice separately, we have all our guys practice and work out together. The tenured veteran gets the same treatment as the rookie.

We even compete at volunteer events. Major bragging rights were on the line for who could mount televisions first at the Community Matters Cafe coffee shop, for who could build children's bicycles the fastest for the Ronald McDonald House, or who could deliver all their lunches and complete their route the fastest for Cabarrus County Meals on Wheels. The local police can attest to our guys' desire to compete because it seems that they have to write a warning every time we perform that event.

A quote we live by comes from social reformer Jacob Riis: "When nothing seems to help, I go look at a stonecutter hammering away at his rock, perhaps a hundred times without as much as a crack showing in it…yet at the hundred and first blow it will split in two and I know it was not that blow that did it, but all that had gone before." By placing such a heavy emphasis on healthy competition, the result is an intentional congruence that weaves itself through everything we do. If you aren't competing, learning, leading, and striking with intention with passionate focus, you will never see successful outcomes in the moments that matter. However, If you are competing and leading in the small things, the things that have nothing to do with championship moments, you will be prepared for the colossal moments, the moments when life demands your absolute best. The rock will split in two. Strike 1 and strike 101 are the same. Quality is always a result.

What You Say Matters

Due to the athleticism, strength, and competitive drive that pitting race cars requires, we get a lot of former athletes who are looking for a spot on our team, especially former football players.

There is a story from one of our guys who tore his ACL twice while playing football at a Division 1 university in North Carolina, a story that impacted us and shaped the way we lead our team. This player worked hard in rehab, stayed focused on his goals, and eventually got back to a place where he was fully healthy and stronger than ever. He was told that he was playing some of the best football he had ever played. However, because the team had picked up a big-time recruit in the off-season to fill his spot, he played on a limited basis. When he asked his coach about his lack of playing time, the coach simply told him, "We promised the recruit and his parents that he was going to be our starter, but we know we have you if we need you. Your chances of ever starting again are unlikely; see you out on the field."

This coach failed to see that the way in which he crafted his words could either inspire great efforts among his players or discourage them. The coach could have inspired this young man instead of discouraging him if he had said, "I made a promise to our starter that I intend to keep, but I want you to show up every day, like I made a promise to you. Success doesn't reward the wrong person. Keep your head and your energy high, and I will get you in as much as I can. Keep growing as a leader, and if you give your best in the classroom and on the field, I promise that we'll look back on our time here with no regrets."

The coach still would have ultimately been telling this player that his playing time would continue to be limited, but he would have inspired him to keep working hard, to help make his teammates better, and to keep preparing himself for any opportunity that could arise at any given moment in an injury-prone sport like football. This seemingly insignificant conversation had the potential to make the team better, but instead, it deflated the player's spirits and made him feel like he didn't even belong on the team. In an environment where everything matters, it seemed that nothing mattered. Regrettably, and to no surprise, this player would rarely go the extra mile in practice. Why would he? It wouldn't make a difference.

That player was Mike Metcalf.

Leaders inevitably have to have difficult conversations with those they are leading. When depicting the realities of a situation or delivering constructive criticism, sometimes it requires telling people information they may not want to hear, information that can evoke disappointment. That's the business of sports, of life. But it can be done in a way that still inspires. It can be done in a way that still informs people that they still have vital roles on the team and inspires them to play those roles as fiercely as their abilities allow.

As a leader, every little thing you say matters. From every team speech you give to every passing conversation you have, from every heat-of-the-moment reaction to every private meeting, from every email or text to every in-depth brainstorming session, your words can either inspire people and positively impact your environment (people, processes, and precedents), or it can cause division, chaos, or frustration.

Which will you choose?

Managing Expectations

Perfectionism creeps up whenever leaders become too focused on meeting their performance expectations. It's a leader's job to inspire the journey and pursuit of excellence rather than trapping others in a prison of their own performance expectations. As tennis legend Mary Browne once said, "Preconceived notions (expectations) are the locks on the doors to wisdom."

That being said, it's no secret that expectations are necessary. There is no sense completely eliminating them. But expectations can either positively fuel a process or person or starve it of joy. Expectations are assets, but they must be managed.

You know by now how immersed we are in time measurements in our racing world. Every individual movement and every two-tenths of a second matters. Our jobs as coaches ultimately hinge on our performance as a team. Our players' jobs ultimately hinge on their individual performance on race day. In areas where performance is so important, it's easy for imprisoning expectations or a demand for perfectionism to creep up and take over. But perfectionism, a lot of times, is related to either fear, ego, or both, and all act as cancers to culture. When you are focusing on the wrong things, it can mentally paralyze you or set you up for failure from the start. Again, when our guys are on the wall for a pit stop, we want them thinking about their fundamentals: lug nuts, stud patterns, fuel capacity, etc., not their jobs or what will happen if they aren't perfect. We want them thinking about excellence, not perfection.

Approach everything with hope, joy, and enthusiasm, but also with the understanding that life does not always unfold the way that dreams do. We once worked with a crew chief who was rather disgruntled because he really wanted to be a driver. Yet he called the shots for a race team, traveled the top racing circuit with the top talent, and made a really good living in the process. He was actually living out his dream, but his expectations clouded his ability to see that. Mismanaged expectations can negatively shift perspective, altering our attention and focus from the things we are accomplishing. Simply put, expectations do not often align with reality. Expectations are not the dream or goal in and of themselves, but rather the cables to help you jump-start the experience of the dream or goal.

Our recommendation is that you DECK your expectations—align your expectations with the four components of the acronym we mentioned earlier:

- **Diverse expectations:** Success shows up in various ways; don't miss the race by parking yourself in one pit box.
- **Efficient expectations:** Adjust your expectations in real time to align them with where you are and where you want to be.
- **Culture expectations:** Similar to an organization, you have your own personal culture to build. Do this by expecting excellence

and placing emphasis on who you are becoming over what you accomplish.
- **Kindness expectations:** As stated, we are in the failure business as pit coaches—failure is coming—and life is no different. Have expectations that allow you to be kind to yourself and to know you are not a disaster when you fall short of expectations. Kind expectations always fuel the greater good. Being kind to others often starts with being kind to yourself.

Think about it. What's more productive: pushing yourself to think, perform, and dream daringly, knowing that failure is coming and that the failure itself will inform you of where you can improve and grow, or trying to perform in a way that is practically perfect and expecting everything to work without flaws? The answer is obvious, yet what do we tend to do? If you are anything like us, we fall short of our expectations all the time, but we've learned to not let them knock us out of the race. In the words of former NFL wide receiver Mohamed Massaquoi, "I've learned the hard way that it's OK when things don't go as planned. Looking back, we've learned that hitting rock bottom, even, is OK. It's life giving you something solid to stand on as you get back into the game."

High-functioning teams don't overwhelm themselves with expectations. Why? The goal isn't to be perfect in the end. It's simply to be better tomorrow.

What's Your Competitive Advantage?

When our team's mechanics and engineers hit on something and somehow find a way to make our race car run a little faster on Sunday, a common saying in the racing industry, is, "You only have a few weeks before everyone else figures out what you're doing." The same is true in pitting race cars.

Whenever we find a way to cut down a couple of movements or further optimize a technique, we know we don't have long before everyone else starts replicating these ideas. We are aware of this because we are watching other teams as well. The data—the faster times—direct competitors toward evaluating the processes that produced the faster times. No matter the age we're living in or the industry, data are constantly being evaluated and dissected, whether they relate to industrial processes, enlightenment, engineering, technology, or social media. Everyone is trying to gain an edge over their competitors. Across the board, analytics is what has always fueled competition and innovation.

But the more that people have access to data, the more leaders need to invest in culture. As educator Peter Drucker so eloquently stated, "Culture eats strategy for breakfast." As important and transformative as data analytics is to a company, you still win with people. Data inform processes, but it's people who put these processes into motion. A business, department, or program becomes self-regulatory whenever pride is infused throughout every seemingly insignificant facet of the operation. Yet that happens only when you have intrinsically motivated people, a rootedness in character and integrity, and a shared vision. It's easier to work with data or cars than people, but analytics only gets you so far.

In *Moneyball: The Art of Winning an Unfair Game*, author Michael Lewis details Oakland Athletics general manager Billy Beane's use of sabermetrics in the late 1990s and 2000s, which is, in short, the detailed analysis of baseball statistics. It gave the cash-strapped team a massive advantage. But now, guess what? Everyone uses sabermetrics. Data are important, but culture is where you gain an advantage. Strategy can be copied. Culture is incredibly difficult to replicate.

In our second year as coaches, we had a young athlete—the one we mentioned earlier who was listening to heavy metal before pitting cars—who had won the competition to be placed on our top-performing car at the start of the season. We could see from the very start that he was exceptionally talented, even though he had had several short stints with many other racing teams. In fact, when coaches from other teams saw that we were starting him, they openly questioned our decision and were even laughing behind our backs. Our pit crew culture, however, created a space for him to fail quickly, have fun, and ultimately excel. Again, all he needed was a change in environment.

After the season ended, a number of pit crew coaches who had been laughing at us at the start of the year approached the kid with contract offers, far higher than anything we could ever offer him. We sat him down and said to him, "We'll never hold anyone here or make anyone feel guilty for leaving, so feel free to go or do whatever you want. But just know that these same people making you offers now were laughing at you and saying we were idiots for putting you on the Cup car at the start of the year. If you do accept one of these offers, just be conscious of the kind of environment they have."

The kid declined every offer and stayed with us. He understood that being in the sun, water, and soil—his environment—as healthy as the one he and his teammates had helped to build was a type of currency that couldn't be topped with dollar signs or prestige. He chose culture over strategy. Culture had become a competitive advantage for him, for us, and a frontier for personal progress. It is a currency all its own.

Kindness Wins

The changers, with securely installed lug nuts, move away from the car to signal a completed pit stop. The jackman drops the jack, looking at the front changer's gun and listening to the rear changer's gun. The carrier wipes dirt, oil, and tire rubber off the front-grill screen to keep the appropriate amount of air going to the radiator and brakes. The gasman prepares to deliver the last half gallon, unplugging the can once the car starts moving. The car only gets "full" when the car is flat. The driver, you, with fresh tires and a full fuel load, re-enters the race after a completed reset.

-The 12th second of a NASCAR pit stop

One exceptionally cold October race day, we were asked to join our driver for an autograph signing outside one of the oldest tracks in NASCAR, the historic Martinsville Speedway. It was scheduled to be a twenty-five-minute session, from 11:35 a.m. to noon. A line of fans had gathered despite the chill in hopes of getting a brief moment with their favorite race car driver. Our pit crew and driver went about efficiently autographing hats, shirts, and chests; taking pictures; and smiling for almost all the fans who had braved the cold.

We wish we were making this up, but at 11:59:59, our driver abruptly stood up and left. Only two people were left in line. *Two people*.

The majority of the fans got what they came for that day, but there were two left brokenhearted. We, the pit crew, did all we could to make that a special moment for them still, but those fans obviously wanted an autograph from the driver. We didn't win the race that day, but the biggest win could have been the 12 seconds of kindness that would have lifted the spirits of two eager fans.

We have also been on a pit crew that saw our driver accidentally run over our tire changer mid-season on a two-tire stop. This tire changers had worked to overcome lots of personal and professional adversity and was now an elite tire changer who had helped this driver win races. After being hit by the car leaving the pit stall, the changer hobbled back to the wall, clearly in pain, only to hear the driver's voice over the headset, "Is the tire changer OK? I didn't see him while I was leaving." Six months into the season, the driver didn't know the changer's name.

We as a society must realize that elevating the needs of others over ourselves and our own agendas is the only way out of the stressed-out, self-centered, and often hateful mess we are in. How long will it take for us to start treating others the way we would like to be treated?

German writer Johann Wolfgang von Goethe once said, "Kindness is the golden chain by which society is bound together." Kindness is muted in many different areas of our society, especially in spaces where ego and ambition tend to run the show, none perhaps more prevalent than the workplace. For decades, education has rallied around fueling the labor force. This, then, makes schooling a primary way of shaping behavior. The workplace is no different. It's an extension of that. For many, the workplace is an avenue for receiving affluence, affirmation, or affection—ego boosts—fueling our addiction to themselves.

There is a well-accomplished crew chief in racing who has plenty of success on the racetrack but has done it at the *expense of* people, not *with* them. We have often heard people say, "I hope his trophies keep him company or make him feel valued on his deathbed because that's all he's going to have at this rate."

Somehow we, as people, must stop attaching our identities solely to what we do and instead start thinking about the role we can play in the lives of others. When our identities are attached to what we do and accomplish, our animating motive will be to elevate ourselves and step on others. But here's the thing: people won't remember you by what you do; people will remember you for how you treated them, for how kind you were, for how you made them feel. If you discover the cure for cancer, maybe you can get away with being a jerk. But generally speaking, when it comes to the legacy you leave, what you accomplished will take a backseat to the person you are and how you treated others.

If you want to leave a legacy as an individual or as a team, simply be kind. That's it.

Be. Kind. Always.

String together days…and then years…and then decades…that are marked by kindness. Everything else will take care of itself. Live a life that is infused with kindness. We couldn't agree more with this anonymous quote: "Perhaps the only legacy worth having is to be known as a kind and compassionate person."

For kindness, the acronym TEAM stands for *transparency, empathy, action,* and *more*. Each are different aspects of kindness that leaders must exemplify if they want those they are leading to be animated by kindness as well. Kindness changes any environment in which it is applied. It is kindness that will change our workplace, our world.

Transparency

One of the more memorable people we have worked with over the course of our careers was a guy who worked in the garage and always sported an intimidating scowl on his face. Whenever we would talk to him one-on-one, however, he was extremely friendly and personable. We would always leave these conversations bewildered, wondering why such a pleasant person would carry himself with such an unwelcoming persona.

One day, one of our tire changers said to him, "What's your deal, man? Why do you always look so pissed off all the time?"

The guy laughed and said, "I try to look like this because I come to work to get things done. If I walk around with a smile on my face, then people like you will want to come up and talk to me. I don't have time for that. I'm here to work."

We love this story because it depicts most workplace postures. There are high schools that teach AP physics and calculus but miss precious opportunities to teach "building meaningful connections with others" or "walking a mile in the shoes of others." Most believe that the sole purpose of the workplace is to simply get things done, not to be known or get to know others while accomplishing work. It's what they've been told and taught to believe about work because it's all their bosses seem to care about as well: doing whatever it takes to reach the company's goals. On the other hand, transparency—letting down your guard and opening yourself up to others—is the gateway to connection. It's the only way you can both give and receive kindness. The man with a scowl could have been going through a difficult time in his life, but no one would have ever known. One conversation with a coworker could have had a big influence on his day—and his life—and let him know he wasn't alone in his struggles. That actually would have helped him be more present with his work and probably ultimately accomplish more. We are more than just our hands and our feet. We are our hearts and our minds. We are our souls.

Yes, there's such a thing as being overly transparent, too, but generally speaking, most in the workplace resemble the man with a scowl: hyper-focused on the tasks that need to be accomplished rather than seeing the opportunity for connection. It goes back to the quote we referenced earlier: "To be 99 percent known is to be unknown."

In any avenue of life where people spend a large portion of their time, like the workplace, most in leadership positions have failed to understand that being open to genuine human connection throughout the day—whether that is a half-hour conversation between two coworkers about life (not working) or spending an afternoon volunteering at a local charity (not working)—will ultimately make their employees more productive because they'll be more centered as humans. A kind culture is a more rewarding and inspiring culture. Constantly isolating yourself or your team "getting things done" doesn't get your culture anywhere. Instead of compartmentalizing the professional from the personal, kindness integrates the human soul into the workplace. Puzzles are completed only with whole pieces. Kindness integrates wholeness.

Empathy

Without question, the most difficult position as a coach is to let go of individuals who have earned your respect. We recently had to let go of two veteran guys who were very dear to us. There were four guys for two spots. Unfortunately, our sport is just like most physically demanding sports: athleticism is everything, eventually your body can't do what it used to do, and there is more supply than demand. Over the years, we wished we could've held on to so many of our guys who positively impacted our environment, but our guys know their careers have an expiration date. Despite the realities of the sport and us trying to prepare them for life after racing, it's hard every time we have to let go of a high-character teammate.

The day we had to announce to these two that they would be released after the next race, we sat in our office with an engineer who had recently been brought in from another racing team to lead the technical aspects of our pit stops (analytics, data, tool improvement, film, video, personnel evaluation, etc.). The two guys we had to release came in separately to talk to us.

The first guy was a long-time tire carrier who started with us as a development guy all the way back at Red Bull. He was an original hire, a guy who was instrumental in our turnaround. We had all been through so much together and had seen the environment change and move forward together in unfathomable ways. And we had seen him move forward in incredible ways in his personal life and development. In a period of five years, he got married, bought a house, and had two beautiful children with his amazing wife. On our team, he became a strong leader whom his teammates looked up to and relied on. It was emotional to be in that office with him and reflect on how far we had seen him come, in both his personal and professional life.

When we delivered the news to him, he responded by saying that he had burned a bridge every time he departed from a team and didn't want to do that with us. He told us that he watched our every move inside and outside of work and that the previous five years changed his life. He said he had been preparing to move on and was ready for the next chapter of life but would give 100 percent in the next race. He thanked us, we thanked him, and we embraced. These moments are difficult enough, but it was even more heart-wrenching in this case because there we were, trying to fire him, and he was telling us he loves and appreciates us.

We immediately had to follow that up by delivering more unfortunate news. We had a tire changer who had been on four teams in three years, and he said that none of them quite felt like home until this last stop—a place where he said that people accepted him. He was very emotional in our meeting, moved to tears. It took him a minute to regain his composure, actually. With previous racing teams, he said he felt like he always had to prove to himself and others that he was one of the best, that he belonged. In this moment of "letting go," it registered that he had actually accomplished just that. He had often felt like an outsider, but he told us that his teammates helped him know that he was accepted for who he was in his uniqueness, not for his performance at the track. He, too, was fully prepared to dive right into his next chapter of life.

After these two difficult conversations, our oldest crew member, a huge culture guy, came in to check on us. We didn't ask him to do that—he just felt and sensed the heaviness of the day when we told the team earlier that we would be finalizing our roster that day. He told us how thankful he was that we did not ask for his input on any of the roster decisions because of how impossible of a decision it was to make. He encouraged us by saying he appreciated how we never play favorites and simply try to bring out the best in everyone, and told us how grateful he was for how we handled difficult days like this. We have made plenty of mistakes during these challenges, but he could tell that we needed a boost of encouragement. He then asked us if we needed anything ourselves, and said he could run practice if we needed time to regroup. We told him we were hanging in there but that we really appreciated him checking in. We were able to hang in there after hard conversations because there were more guys like him, Kenyatta, waiting on us.

Our engineer, who had been sitting next to us the whole time, then looked at us and said, "I've seen plenty of people get let go during my time in racing, but I've never seen anything like that before," referring to those last thirty minutes of emotion.

He was struck by the empathy that was apparent in the room, that we all had for one another. Our empathy for the guys we had to move on from, theirs for us, and our veteran tire changers' empathy and awareness to seek us out after letting them go. Our engineer had championship rings himself. He had spent several years working at Joe Gibbs Racing (JGR), led by Joe Gibbs, a Super Bowl and NASCAR Cup Series champion—a guy familiar with winning and success. JGR had more money and resources than we did, multiple championship drivers, and more "talented" pit crew guys because of their budget (according to rankings, but our guys beg to differ). But he had never seen empathy on display like that before. In the midst of tough conversations, kindness was king.

Leaders in corporate America have long considered empathy a sign of weakness. We have the same issue at NASCAR—those with empathy are often thought of as "soft" or lacking competitive fire. But empathy is not a weakness. In fact, emerging schools of thought believe empathy is actually a superpower! Empathy is the driving force behind a healthy environment. If empathy is a scary word for you in your performance-driven world, where there are all kinds of demands and deadlines placed on you, it is because you misunderstand what empathy means. Empathy does not mean tolerating poor performance; it means understanding and connecting with the human factors that drive efficiency so you can move forward, together, as a team. Without empathy, there's no understanding or genuine connection. When leaders do not express empathy, those they are leading can feel isolated because their worth as humans is not being validated. Again, people are more than machines.

Empathy is about being aware enough to enter other people's worlds. Transparency can also make way for empathy because with transparency, needs are named and acknowledged. Empathy is true compassion. It's truly your soul investing in someone else's and connecting with someone else's. It's not enough to say, "I'm sorry to hear that"—true empathy involves entering that space and slowing down enough on an individual level for genuine connection to unfold…for the hurting person to feel heard, understood, and as if his or her pain has been validated.

Empathy isn't expressed just in the big things, like when someone is going through a traumatic situation or dealing with loss in some way. Empathy extends into the small things. It's absurd when people in the workplace don't feel the need to thank their janitorial staff or secretary or behind-the-scenes people.

You'd be surprised how much you can positively impact people in your workplace just by simply meeting them in their struggles and letting them know they aren't alone. It doesn't take much. For example, on one of the past racing teams, we had a wonderful Human Resources lady who went out of her way for everyone. She was a classic example of someone whose work was often overlooked because she was so integral in everything and always did such a good job that everyone took her efforts for granted. One evening, she was involved in a terrible car wreck. EMTs had to cut her out of her mangled vehicle. It was a miracle that she lived, and it took her a year's worth of therapy to walk normally again. She was obviously bound to a hospital bed in the days following the crash, and the only person from work who went to see her, at a company of 150 people, was someone from the pit crew department who wasn't traveling for the race that day. Her immediate boss didn't visit her. Her immediate boss's boss didn't visit her. Her departmental coworkers didn't visit her. The only person who did was someone from a completely different department. To this day, whenever she shares the story about that person walking through those doors to spend some time with her, she always gets emotional.

The general posture in the American workplace is compartmentalization. Whenever people at a company go through personal trials, so many of their coworkers and bosses have this general attitude: "We're here to make money, not talk about our feelings." Could it be possible that empathy—elevating the humanity of each person and therefore his or her personal highs and lows—taps into who we each innately are, cultivates togetherness, multiplies a deep sense of meaning on a team, integrates the personal with the professional, and ultimately inspires a more positive and efficient culture?

The truth is that if you are too busy to reach out to someone at your company who is struggling, then you are too busy to lead. If someone who you are leading is hurting and you don't notice, then maybe you are placing more emphasis on managing than leading. Maybe you're just good at your job. If someone you are leading is hurting and you know it and you *still* refrain from empathy, then you definitely aren't a leader. You're just a boss. A manager. An executive. Simply doing your job isn't making you a better leader. Good leaders and coaches recognize the wholeness of every person they are leading—their personal lives, their professional lives, everything. They don't compartmentalize. They integrate. A true leader has the empathetic capacity to meet others where they are, in both their lowest places and in their daily challenges.

Action

Transparency gives kindness a chance. Empathy puts kindness into motion. But kindness is ultimately most profoundly displayed through action. The vulnerability of letting oneself be known—transparency—must also lead to daring to know others. Allowing oneself to feel empathy must lead to entering other people's worlds and helping them.

There is a Buddhist parable called "Translating the Word" about a young woman named Sophia who received a vision in which God asked her to dedicate her life to translating and distributing the "Word of God" throughout her country. Bibles were written only in Latin and were used only by the church. She spent fifteen years sharing her vision and begging people for money to build a printing press and purchase the necessary equipment. She slowly but surely gathered all the money she needed.[11]

Right before she was able to break ground on building the printing press, however, a massive flood destroyed a nearby town. Sophia took all the money she had raised and used it to help people rebuild their homes in the flooded town. Then she spent the next nine years raising money once again for the printing press, never forgetting the vision she had received. Once again, the money slowly accumulated. But that was when devastation struck again, this time by a plague that fell upon the city. She once again put the plans for the printing press aside and used her energy and resources to serve the city in its state of emergency. Once the plague had passed, she set out once more to translate the Word of God, never forgetting the vision she had received, though by now she was much older and very ill.[12]

The parable concludes with these words: "Finally, shortly before her death, Sophia was able to gather together the money required for the printing press, the building, and the translators. Although, she was, by this time, close to death, Sophia lived long enough to see the first Bibles printed and distributed. It is said to this day that Sophia had actually accomplished her task of translating and distributing the Word of God three times during her life rather than simply once—the first

---

[11]. "Translating the Word," from the Cosmic Egg blog post by Michael Manley, April 30, 2014, https://michaeldmanley.wordpress.com/2014/04/30/translating-the-word/.
[12]. Ibid.

two being more beautiful and radiant than the last."[13]

The parable is a critique of hypocritical religious people who hide behind doctrine and statements of belief and don't live out what they preach, but it's just as applicable to workplace environments. In our marketing age, a public relations team can spin any story or post anything on social media to convey the image they want others to see. Like Sophia, a company's true identity is revealed through *action*. The actions of an organization are a communication tool in their own right, to their employees, to their teams/departments, and to their consumers. Action speaks volumes.

It's one thing to say that you care about your people; it's another to put action behind it—like Polydeck in South Carolina. The company has a Chief Caring Officer on the senior-level executive staff whose responsibilities include supporting employees through challenging life events, providing counseling services, reinvesting money into the local community, and, above all, ensuring that employees are cared for beyond the services they provide to the company.

When we speak to leaders at companies, one of the first things we say to them is that we aren't there to help them polish their managerial acumen. Instead, we are there to inspire them as leaders. There are plenty of programs, masked with leadership lingo, that focus on managing people and managing processes, with the primary goal of attaining financial success. We are trying to take things a step further and inspire leaders to reclaim the soul of the workplace by flipping the entire value structure on its head—where the wholeness of an individual is elevated above the processes that have been implemented for productivity. If managers want to become leaders, then the art of genuine relationships in the workplace must be reclaimed. When relationships are reclaimed, servant leadership and profound action naturally unfold. Vulnerability and empathy flow out of genuine relationships, almost always leading to action because you realize you are connected to (and responsible for) the person next to you.

When relationships are elevated, what you begin to notice is that everyone has been affected by something on a deep, personal level, whether it's drunk driving or homelessness or chronic illness or domes-

---

[13] Ibid.

tic abuse or having a family member serve in the military. The workplace can become an avenue for service, whether it's volunteering at Alcoholics Anonymous or a homeless shelter or a local hospital or a shelter for battered women or Wounded Warriors. The elevation of people *inside* the workplace leads to the elevation of people *outside* the workplace. Simply said, "work" isn't "designed" to bring fulfillment. But fulfillment can quickly come into an organization that gets behind a cause that is near and dear to someone's heart. That person having space to heal and help make a difference for someone else absolutely brings fulfillment and connection to others. Reclaiming personhood creates purpose and perspective.

Team members will come and go. Old racing teams will fold. New racing teams will form. Teams will transition and transform. There will be winning seasons and losing seasons. But what we did as a team with regard to human connection—whether it's mowing a widow's lawn, going on a retreat together, taking truckloads of bikes to Ronald McDonald House, having deep conversations at work, laughing uncontrollably at work, volunteering at Charlotte Rescue Mission, or simply giving a teammate space to have his final moments with a dying family member without having to think about work—will live on forever. The work will always be there, baiting us with its superficial importance. We are the first to admit that we have made plenty of decisions in our coaching careers that have been incorrect, and we know we have made plenty of performance mistakes. But we want to be able to look back on our body of work and say, "We did this the *right* way." People won't generally remember the trophies, the hats, or the brand of victory champagne. People will forget the bonuses they got. But people carry with them memories of how they interacted with people.

What's the one thing you can do today to be kinder in your relationships with others and in your career? Let us know at info@deckleadership.com. How can you elevate human connection more in your life and in the workplace?

More

Kindness is never a bad thing. It's not illegal. There are no limits to it. You don't need more money or resources to be kind right where you are now. You hardly ever hear anyone say, "I'm being too kind right now." We can always be kinder to ourselves, and we can always be kinder to others. We're so hard on ourselves, and we're so judgmental of others. The kinder you are, the more meaningful your life will be.

Don't hear us wrong. Trophies and numbers are important—they *do* tell the story of your productivity and efficiency as an organization. Kindness alone might not make your organization successful. But entrenching your pursuit of excellence with kindness will position your team to experience both success and a deep sense of meaning along the way. The best teams in racing initially were the ones who had a mechanical advantage, and then the best teams were those with an engineering advantage. Decades later, mechanics and engineering are all pretty close now. The dominant teams now are the ones with the least divisive environment—a cultural advantage. The next era will be dominated by the teams who are the kindest.

The workplace is filled with people who have crab-like mentalities instead of ant-like mentalities. If you were to put a bunch of crabs in a bucket and one of them started to climb its way out toward the rim, the other crabs, trying to pull themselves out, would end up pulling each other back down into the bucket. Ants, on the other hand, are always connected to each other and will climb great heights by supporting each other. For ants, the agenda of the *colony* outweighs the agenda of the *one*. Our culture in America is incredibly individualized; we prefer crabs over ants. But kindness gets us back to who we were made to be: back to our connectedness with all people.

We hope to play a small role in a movement that puts kind people in leadership positions—which is ultimately going to be the most efficient way to get the most out of human capital. Every company in this country is digging for gold in some way, but many of them are trying to do it by using fear as the shovel and pickaxe. This isn't empowered digging. It's the equivalent of asking employees to dig for gold on rock-hard desert ground with small, rusted shovels. It's hard work and toil—inching along for a paycheck—but that's it. If we really want to strike gold, we need something more than fear. We need transparency, empathy, and connectedness. Dig with the wholeness of people, not fragments. Lead with kindness, and you'll find that those you are leading will be inspired to unlock their own creativity, innovation, and uniqueness and be fully present with the task at hand—the equivalent of digging with high-powered, million-dollar machinery.

The initial manuscript of this book contained thirty-nine chapters and was categorized in the four parts of DECK: diversity, efficiency, culture, and kindness. What we realized, however, is that the components of DECK are too difficult to categorize individually because of how they overlap and inform one another. Hopefully you could feel that every chapter was saturated with the components of DECK.

We hope something in this book inspired you to see *diversity* a different way. With your support, we'll be back with more on diversity and how it can break chains that have tied down the opportunities that exist in unity. We hope concepts like failing quickly, learning to pivot, and P=W/T inspire you to approach *efficiency* with more power and clarity. We hope that being united around uniqueness, elevating relationships, and inspiring people to go on the search for their best selves might move your *culture* forward in a new way, a brilliant way.

It is easy to get excited about diversity, efficiency, and culture, but it's *kindness* that completes the square of DECK.

Most company buildings are architecturally constructed around the building block of the right angle. That's why the foundation of most buildings and skyscrapers contains four sides. Don't forget the four corners of DECK and the kindness piece that will complete the foundation of your company, team, or department so you can build it higher and higher. Kindness will take you to greater heights because there is always *more* kindness to give.

Kindness begins in dignity. *Imago Dei* is a theological term that means "Image of God." No matter how you feel about religion, daring to believe that every person is made in the image of God—that their hearts and minds are unique and bursting with gifts and ideas, that they have a best self within them ready to be unleashed in the right environment—is a healthy starting place for kindness.

Snowflakes are perfectly beautiful, intricate, and unique—no snowflake is the same. Focusing on the remarkable detail of a single snowflake can inspire wonder and awe within you. Kindness is kind of like contemplating the mystery of a snowflake. Kindness is relational—it leads you to focus on the inherent dignity, remarkable complexity, and wonderful fullness of the person you touch with your act of kindness. Just as staring at a snowflake might help you see your connectedness with the world, being kind helps you see your connectedness with humanity. If we can talk so majestically about a snowflake, what could we say about you, your career, your life? What could one small act of kindness do? It could unleash the uniqueness or best self of someone who goes on to change your company or, better yet, the world.

Martin Luther King Jr., once gave a speech, not outlining a plan but rather a dream. What dream do you have or could you have about today and tomorrow? NASCAR races begin and end in the same place—the start–finish line. What actions have you stopped that you could start? What have you started that you need to stop?

We thought we had lucked our way into a career in motorsports because we were passionate about competing and racing. This is partially true. We love competing in races, aspiring to always be the fastest on pit road, but we are more passionate about the race we are all in together—the human race. Our frustrations provide the daily fuel, and the biggest frustration we have is how awful we as fellow humans can treat each other. We are all born of a woman, naked and with nothing. We all die and take nothing with us. There is a small dash between the date you are born and the date on which you take your last breath. Our starts and finishes are all the same. The dash between those dates—that's the race, your opportunity to move the collective dash, the human race, forward.

Again, we hope you race with diverse motors along the way. We hope you find the most efficient pathway to success. We hope you build a culture that inspires brilliance all around you. But most of all, the entire world hopes that no matter the situation you're in—whether it's enduring a tough meeting, sitting in traffic, raising toddlers, or improving trying relationships—you'll be kind.

When you look into the rear-view mirror of the life you have lived and the race you have been driving, a great race will have been a kind one. Achieving the American Dream won't give you the race you want, but kindness will. Treat people with kindness. Be a kind interaction. We left this last second at twelve…because if you are reading this, you are still in the race.

How it ends is up to you.

About the Authors

Mike Metcalf, being the oldest of four siblings, learned the struggles of leadership at an early age. The Charlotte native and former football student-athlete graduated with honors from Appalachian State University. He first entered the world of motorsports in 2006 as a member of a NASCAR pit crew. Mike quickly climbed the ranks and started coaching pit crews, in addition to competing in 2012. Currently, he is co-head coach for the Chip Ganassi Racing Pit Crew Department and fuel man for the No. 42 team. Outside motorsports, Mike is active in the community. He serves on the board of directors for The Daddy Saturday Foundation in Charleston, South Carolina, and RunningWorks in Charlotte, North Carolina. His hobbies include yoga, traveling, eating, meeting new people, and most importantly, spending time with his wife and children.

Shaun Peet was born and raised on Vancouver Island, Canada. He came to the United States on a hockey scholarship and played four years in the Ivy League at Dartmouth College. While at Dartmouth, he graduated with high honors and a double major in psychology and sociology. He went on to play eight years in the minor leagues, serving as the captain of the New Mexico Scorpions before his career culminated with an opportunity to play for the Calder Cup with the American League's Wilkes-Barre Scranton Penguins. A chance meeting with a fan afforded him an opportunity to work in NASCAR as a Jackman on a pit crew for the next sixteen years, as a part of the Red Bull Racing Crew that won the 2008 World Pit Crew Championships. In 2013, he was approached to coach the Chip Ganassi Pit Crew Department. He resides in Davidson, North Carolina, with his wife, Jane.

Real People. Real Stories.

CORE

You have a story that is worth sharing, a story that the world needs to hear. Let us help you!
Learn more at www.thecoremediagroup.com.

For questions about books or other inquiries, please contact info@thecoremediagroup.com.

FOLLOW US

The Core Media Group, Inc.
@SpiritInStory